MAKE

ALL AMERICA

A

SCHOOL

SECOND EDITION

Make All America a School™

MIND EXTENSION UNIVERSITY®
THE EDUCATION NETWORK™

SECOND EDITION

GLENN R. JONES

JONES 21ST CENTURY™, INC.
ENGLEWOOD, COLORADO

PUBLISHED BY JONES 21ST CENTURY™, INC.,
A DIVISION OF
JONES INTERNATIONAL™, LTD.
9697 E. MINERAL AVENUE, ENGLEWOOD, CO 80112

ISBN: 0-945373-023

TABLE OF CONTENTS

i

DEDICATION

The *Jones Dictionary of CATV Terminology, Second Edition,* published in 1973, was dedicated to the concept of access to the knowledge of humankind. "Quick access from the home or office." And to the cable TV industry I said, "Make it happen."

In the dedication to the third edition, it was noted:

> Ever-increasing amounts of new information and entertainment bombard us from every side, every day. The mind simply cannot manage the onslaught by itself.
>
> By utilizing the electronic pipeline called cable television and associated technologies, there is hope that we can attain one of humankind's greatest achievements: the dramatic extension of the human mind.

The dictionary was dedicated to the role that cable can play in that quest.

In dedicating this book, I re-embrace these prior dedications and focus on a specific thing we can do, now:

MAKE ALL AMERICA A SCHOOL.

A school available to all regardless of their station in life. A school where equality of educational opportunity exists. A school that is a place of excitement. Where hope is alive. A place where the clash of technologies and the maelstrom of ideas are orchestrated to the service of education. A place that sees the wilderness of information as our new frontier.

Make all America a school. We can do it, now.

Glenn R. Jones

iii

FOREWORD

As educators we embrace the conviction that education must be viewed as a lifelong process. As a society we are increasingly cognizant of the fact that individuals do not cease learning upon receiving a high school or college diploma. In fact, graduation ceremonies are commencement exercises. They are beginnings of a continuing journey of learning.

This journey assumes a greater sense of urgency and importance when we note that many adults will change employment and careers several times during their lifetimes. Thus, the acquisition of new skills will be ever present for a significant proportion of the population, and the demand for education will be continuous. Meeting this demand is, of course, one of the challenges we face as educators.

Coupled with the necessity of providing continuing educational opportunities for a growing and increasingly older proportion of the population is the requirement to better serve the many youngsters who are currently in our schools and who, for a variety of reasons, are unsuccessful. The tragedy of this situation is that the failure of these youngsters in school deprives the nation of a cadre of individuals our society will need as we face the future. Whereas many approaches have been posited to address the school failure of large groups of students, it may well be that technology represents a resource of great potential for reversing this situation. Through the use of computers, interactive TV, teleconferencing, telecourses, televised instruction, and the like, the potential for effectively providing an educational delivery system in which all students will be successful is greatly enhanced.

These themes dominate the present opus. The author provides the rationale for the use of technology for educational access and skillfully describes the technological approaches available to the educational community, using Mind Extension University as a focal point.

As educators, as parents, and as citizens, we must consider the use of every available tool to improve educational opportunity and the acquisition of knowledge. Jones' discussion of the use of technology in this regard provides a good entrée to this world.

Rodney J. Reed
Dean, College of Education and
    Pennsylvania Professor of Education
The Pennsylvania State University

INTRODUCTION

Mind Extension University (ME/U), an education network discussed in this book, is an electronic tool. It focuses on higher, for-credit education, but offers pre-college and self-enrichment education as well. It was christened Mind Extension University because mind extension is the core of an information society. Mind Extension University is an entrepreneur's approach to educational needs, and it is a tool we enthusiastically bend to the purposes of education, self-government and the progress of civilization.

Since Socrates first addressed the nature of knowledge, educators have struggled with two central questions: what to teach and how to teach it. The debate echoes from antiquity and volleys across today's academic journals, government reports, business magazines, and mainstream best-sellers. Exploding beyond the borders of education and legislatures, the debate is now being enacted in town halls, corporate boardrooms, and even dining rooms throughout America and other countries. The concept behind Mind Extension University, that of delivering education to people instead of people to education, contributes yet another question to the debate: *where* should the learning take place?

In America, how these questions are answered has special significance because the answers will have a major impact on our youthful, vibrant and continuing experiment with self-government. As historians Will and Ariel Durant pointed out more than two decades ago in *Lessons of History,* access to education is the key:

> If equality of educational opportunity can be established, democracy will be real and justified. For this is the vital truth beneath its catchwords: that though men cannot be equal, their access to educational opportunity can be made more nearly equal.[1]

Our culture has undergone a transformation that lends great urgency to these questions. This transformation is our headlong emergence into an information society. This emergence has created a sense that we are out of control. Decision-makers, who must in any event make decisions, are deluged with information they cannot grasp and with choices they do not comprehend. Everything is moving with great speed. There seems to be nothing to hold on to.

The information society we have entered differs greatly from the industrial society we leave behind. In the industrial society the principal resource was energy, and its tools were artifacts like forklifts, cranes, trucks, trains, automobiles, and airplanes. Its principal characteristic was that it allowed us to extend the human body.

The information society is different because the velocity of its evolution is much more rapid and its principal resource is information. Information is a special kind of resource. It can be weightless, invisible, and in many different places at once. The tools of the information society drive the creation, storage, delivery, manipulation, and transformation of that information. Importantly, the principal characteristic of the information revolution is that it allows us to dramatically extend the human mind.

The quantum extension of the human mind combined with the ability to extend the human body has resulted in a new reality. A reality in which the human mind, excluding religion and acts of nature, is now more clearly the most powerful force on the planet.

We are all embedded in this evolution, and education has an important part to play. Education is how information becomes meaningful. Information without meaning is useless. Education converts information into knowledge, understanding, and wisdom much like temperature turns water into ice. Education is the loom through which information is woven into value systems, dignity, self-worth, freedom and into civilization itself.

Again, Will and Ariel Durant stated it well:

> If education is the transmission of civilization, we are unquestionably progressing. Civilization is not inherited; it has to be learned and earned by each generation anew; if transmission should be interrupted for one century, civilization would die, and we should be savages again. So our finest contemporary achievement is our unprecedented expenditure of wealth and toil in the provision of higher education for all.[2]

The issue is well stated in clear economic terms by William B. Johnston and Arnold H. Packer in their landmark study *Workforce 2000*, a Hudson Institute publication on the future of the American economy and workers:

> Education and training are the primary systems by which the human capital of a nation is preserved and increased. The speed and efficiency with which these education systems transmit knowledge governs the rate at which human capital can be developed. Even more than such closely-watched indicators as the rate of investment in plant and equipment, human capital formation plays a direct role in how fast the economy can grow.[3]

It is the obligation and opportunity of every person and organization committed to the concept of self-government and to the forward progress of civilization to lend what tools they can to assist in the education of humankind. The questions are what, how, and where to teach for optimum benefit. Optimum benefit to individual learners, to the concept of self-government, and to the forward progress of civilization.

[1]Will and Ariel Durant, *The Lessons of History* (New York: Simon and Schuster, 1968), p. 79. See also the discussion of democracy and education on pp. 77-79.

[2]Durant, *Lessons of History,* p. 101.

[3]William B. Johnston and Arnold H. Packer, *Workforce 2000: Work and Workers for the Twenty-first Century* (Indianapolis, Ind.: Hudson Institute, 1987), p. xxvii.

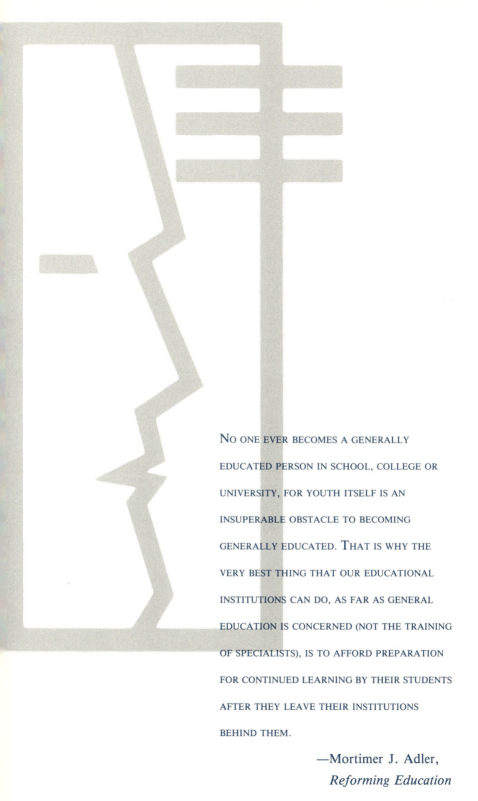

No one ever becomes a generally educated person in school, college or university, for youth itself is an insuperable obstacle to becoming generally educated. That is why the very best thing that our educational institutions can do, as far as general education is concerned (not the training of specialists), is to afford preparation for continued learning by their students after they leave their institutions behind them.

—Mortimer J. Adler,
Reforming Education

MIND EXTENSION UNIVERSITY
The Education Network™

A CHANGING ENVIRONMENT

The demographic and social changes that have been developing over the past three decades are now having a strong impact on our entire education system. For example, our past assumptions about who the "typical" college student was as well as how, when, why, and where that student attended college are no longer valid. Today our colleges and universities are faced with new facts.

As a society we are changing our view of education. We no longer define a college education as something we do between the ages of 18 and 22; we are coming to understand and embrace the concept of "lifelong learning."[1]

Ken Dychtwald and Joe Flower in their book *Age Wave* described this changing approach to education:

> You may stop working one or more times in your thirties, forties, or fifties in order to go back to school, raise a second (or third) family, enter a new business, or simply to take a couple of years to travel and enjoy yourself. You may go back to work in your sixties, seventies, or even eighties. You may find that the traditional framework of life—with youth the time for learning, adulthood for non-stop working and raising a family, and old age for retirement—will come unglued, offering new options at every state. A cyclic life arrangement will replace the current linear life plan as people change direction and take up new challenges many times in their lives.[2]

In fact, numerous studies undertaken in the past several years by industry groups, the government, public institutions, and private foundations are projecting that by the year 2020 the average worker will undergo *at least* five major job changes in his or her lifetime.

ISSUES IN HIGHER EDUCATION

CHANGING STUDENT POPULATION

Enrollment of the "traditional student" at America's colleges and universities is dwindling. As late as 1979, traditional full-time students, 18-22 years old and usually straight out of high school, numbered 4.5 million. By 1992, enrollment of traditional students is expected to fall from the 1979 high to 3.1 million, a decline of 32 percent.[3]

As traditional students represent less and less of higher education's student body, adult learners are stepping in to fill the void. These students are typically 25-35 years old and are employed at least part-time. Many of them have employers who are paying for some or all of their education costs. These students deal with scheduling conflicts, difficulties in getting to campus, geographic relocation brought on by job transfers, and frequently the extra demands of parenthood.

Adult learners typically have little interest in the expensive "extras" of college such as social and athletic events, association with sororities or fraternities, and various other on-campus organizations and activities. Their needs are primarily for flexible scheduling, affordable prices, and attendance options. Such students exist in all types and levels of education, and they are found virtually all around the globe.

ACCESS TO EDUCATION

Access to higher education for geographically distant students, those who must travel, and others who cannot attend campus-held classes is becoming a higher priority for the country. As Americans perceive the importance of a college education to their careers, to their quality of life, to our economy, and to their children's futures, they are becoming increasingly concerned about universal access to higher education. This point is dramatically made by Johnston and Packer in *Workforce 2000* in their prediction that:

> During the 1985-2000 period, the good fortune to be born in or to immigrate to the United States will make less difference than the luck or initiative to be well-educated and well-trained. For individuals, the good jobs of the future will belong to those who have skills that enable them to be productive in a high-skill, service economy. For the nation, the success with which the workforce is prepared for high-skilled jobs will be an essential ingredient in maintaining a high-productivity, high-wage economy.[4]

TEACHER SHORTAGES

Another change affecting higher education is the teacher shortage predicted for at least the next two decades. In their recently published *Prospects for Faculty in the Arts and Sciences*[5], co-authors William Bowen and Julie Ann Sosa confirm what educators have suspected for several years: by the late nineties, a substantially increasing rate of enrollments in higher education will result in major shortages of faculty members at colleges throughout the nation.

As the children of the 77 million baby boomers move through our colleges and universities, they will expand demand for faculty at the same time that many professors, hired to meet the baby boom demand of the 1950s and 1960s, are scheduled to retire. Unless a means is found for delivering education to more students without radically increasing the demand for added faculty, many would-be students will be closed out of the higher education system. At a time when our global competitors are exploiting every opportunity to seize existing markets and outrace us to new ones, the nation cannot afford an undereducated workforce. The productivity of America is at risk; our competitive edge is at stake.

COST INCREASES

Perhaps the most pressing concern regarding higher education is the astounding increase in the costs of attending college.[6] Recent surveys have found that the cost of higher education during the first seven years of the eighties rose 81 percent for private institutions, 61 percent for public universities.[7] These costs continue to outdistance inflation. This rapid increase in cost effectively denies educational opportunity to those unable to afford its escalating expense.

These statistics represent a national crisis: education is one of the few industries in America that is becoming less rather than more productive. This is not a minor issue, since the higher education segment alone employs some two million people, a third of them faculty members, and annually enrolls nearly 12.5 million students. Thus about six percent of the American population either works or studies within the higher education structure.

Part of the problem with costs relates to the expansion and upgrading undertaken by American colleges and universities in the past two decades. This was necessary in order to meet the growing enrollment of baby boom students and to remain academically competitive. In its quest for quality, however, the higher education system has invested in advanced technology and costly physical plants that often sit unused for four to five months each year. This problem will worsen as residence halls, no longer filled with traditional college-age students, have even more empty space that continues to incur maintenance costs.

WORKER RETRAINING

Businesses and labor leaders are recognizing the importance of retraining American workers so that their skills meet twenty-first century employment needs.[8] As the industrial and manufacturing base in the United States continues to erode, the knowledge economy continues to grow. Although the definition of what constitutes "information work" is undergoing continued re-evaluation, there is now a consensus that nearly fifty percent of American workers are employed in some aspect of the "knowledge" or "information" economy.[9] Consequently, our competitive edge in what is now a global marketplace will be based on our ability to teach our workers not just to be technically proficient, but to think, to evaluate, to adapt, to use information resources, and to become lifelong learners.

These skills will be critical in all areas of American industry, not just among top-level management. Without question, this will be a massive undertaking. Equally without question, it is crucial to our ability to maintain an international competitive edge.

Economists estimate that as many as 30 million people have been dislocated by the "restructuring" in manufacturing during the last decade. In his *Thriving on Chaos,* Tom Peters notes that "since 1980, the Fortune 500 have shed a staggering 2.8 million jobs."[10] More restructuring will take place as these companies respond to marketplace demand and competitive threats.

The changing nature and skill requirements of the American workplace have been comprehensively documented by Johnston and Packer in *Workforce 2000*:

> As the economies of developed nations move further into the post-industrial era, human capital plays an ever-more-important role in their progress. As the society becomes more complex, the amount of education and knowledge needed to make a productive contribution to the economy becomes greater.[11]

Later in their analysis, Johnston and Packer state:

> The jobs that will be created between 1987 and 2000 will be substantially different from those in existence today. A number of jobs in the least-skilled job classes will disappear, while high-skilled professions will grow rapidly. Overall, the skill mix of the economy will be moving rapidly upscale, with most new jobs demanding more education and higher levels of language, math and reasoning skills....Among the fastest-growing jobs, the trend toward higher educational requirements is striking. Of all the new jobs that will be created over the 1983-2000 period, more than half will require some education beyond high school, and almost a third will be filled by college graduates. Today, only 22 percent of all occupations require a college degree.[12]

Clearly, new tools and concepts are required to master this rampant change in our environment. Higher levels of education are imperative.

The turbulence of change and the necessity of adjusting are manifest. Yet, for the worker who needs retraining, the military man or woman, the rural adult learner, the gifted high school student with no opportunity to take college-level classes at his or her local high school, shift workers, homebound parents, and various others, access to educational opportunities generally and to college coursework and credit specifically has been difficult, if not impossible.

ISSUES IN ELEMENTARY AND SECONDARY EDUCATION

As our higher education institutions have grappled with shifting circumstances, America's elementary and secondary schools have also had to chart new territory. They have been attempting to meet two important goals: enriching the classroom experience and providing access to a wide and varied education. In addition, these two issues, frequently referred to as "excellence and equity," have been accompanied by a host of other considerations.

STATE-MANDATED CHANGES

New, state-mandated changes in curriculum call for more breadth and depth in courses that schools, particularly at the secondary level, are required to offer. These reforms effect schools of every town, city, county, and school district in America.

Requirements for high school graduation have been radically upgraded in many states, with special emphasis placed on mathematics, science, and languages. State colleges and universities across the country are also emphasizing the importance of these subjects by elevating admission requirements in these areas. Unfortunately, the task of meeting requirements at both the secondary and college levels is aggravated by a shortage of appropriate teachers and budgetary pressures.

In addition to the curricular changes called for, most states now require teachers to participate in professional development or in-service training courses on a regular basis. However, for many teachers such courses are unavailable, inaccessible, or at best inconvenient. Yet the importance of professional development cannot be underestimated. To keep pace with the expanding educational requirements of their students, teachers must stay current with the most recent advances in their fields.

Low national test scores and the poor showing of American students relative to students from other nations are more than discomforting. Our students are confronting the onslaught of an information age, and the cry for change is clear and compelling.

TEACHER SHORTAGES AND
BUDGET CONSTRAINTS

As noted in *Linking for Learning,* the report on distance education issued in 1989 by the Department of Commerce's Office of Technology Assessment,

> Shifting economic and demographic patterns have left many small and rural schools with declining student populations and even more limited financial and instructional resources. ...Solutions such as school consolidation or transporting students or teachers have often been stretched to their geographic limits; these approaches are also disruptive and politically unpopular.[13]

Yet these schools must provide the basics of a good education and, if possible, broaden their students' intellectual exposure beyond the confines of their immediate locale.

Struggling to provide a basic education to all students, many schools have few remaining resources with which to meet the unique needs of individuals who either have difficulty learning or are intellectually gifted students. This is especially true for schools located in areas that are culturally isolated, economically disadvantaged, or both.

When resources must be stretched to address the needs of the majority of students, there is a painful recognition that gifted students, some of whom perhaps have the potential to provide signature insights about our world and its problems, may go unchallenged. This is a painful situation because unless such students are challenged early, their ability to see unique relationships and to optimize their conceptualizing skills may be lost forever.

Teacher shortages are yet another area of concern. The current shortage of qualified teachers in three key areas—math, science, and languages—is projected to worsen dramatically over the next two decades. For lack of a better alternative, some secondary schools have resorted to hiring teachers to teach subjects for which they are less than fully prepared. Finding teachers qualified to teach English as a second language is particularly critical in many locations.

This problem is shared by both rural and urban schools. Often schools cannot afford the luxury of hiring teachers for courses such as trigonometry or Latin if only a few students will enroll. And some schools cannot convince subject-qualified teachers to relocate to their geographic area.

The ongoing dilemma of whether to focus financial and teaching resources on breadth or depth in the curriculum presents yet another problem for America's schools. Struggling with budget and personnel constraints, many schools must choose between offering their students an extensive, broad-based curriculum that covers a large number of subjects lightly or an intensive, highly focused curriculum that covers key subjects in depth but other areas only superficially, if at all.

This dilemma cuts to the heart of the curricular reform debate: will a broad-based, general education or a more focused (for example, concentration on math and science) education better prepare students for the world they will face as adults? Although proponents for both sides of the debate have present-ed compelling rationales over the past several years, most educators still believe the goal is to find a way to offer both breadth and depth, ensuring the most comprehensive educational grounding possible.

DISTANCE EDUCATION:
AN INNOVATIVE SOLUTION

As social, demographic, and financial changes developed over the past three decades, leaders in education worked to fashion new responses to these changing circumstances. Some of the most successful of the evaluated programs involved distance education, a form of instruction in which the student is linked to the school through a faculty member, but is not necessarily attending regular classes on campus or even in a classroom. Essentially, learning takes place "at a distance."

Of the distance education alternatives, telecourses, or televised instruction, proved to be one of the most promising. Advances in communications technologies such as cable television, fiber optics, microwave, slow-scan television, satellites, microcomputer networks, fax machines and videocassette recorders (VCRs) have allowed telecourse design and delivery to become even more effective.

DEVELOPMENT OF TELECOURSES

Telecourses have been part of this country's educational delivery system since television classes were first broadcast into America's homes more than 30 years ago. Typically received by ordinary home antennas from local broadcast television stations, these early, rudimentary telecourses brought traditional classroom presentations directly into the student's living room.

Chicago Citywide College, an extension of the City College of Chicago, took the lead in testing and developing this new education delivery system.[14] Supported by a grant from the Ford Foundation's Fund for Advancement of Education, Chicago Citywide College began broadcasting telecourses over Chicago's public educational television station, WTTW, in 1956. From those early days of trial-and-error experimentation, Chicago Citywide College has continued its commitment to expand the applicability and enhance the effectiveness of telecourse instruction. And, although many other colleges have since followed its lead, Chicago Citywide's program is generally recognized to have set the stage for the educational television we have today.

While Chicago Citywide College was establishing itself, another Ford Foundation-supported project for television in higher education was begun at The Pennsylvania State University, also in 1956. The purpose of the Penn State project was to explore the potential use of closed-circuit television for on-campus instruction. A successful undertaking, the project had produced twenty-eight courses for the university by 1966.

Widespread experimentation with telecourses continued through the sixties, seventies, and eighties, with Michigan State University (East Lansing, Mich.), American University (Washington, D.C.), Case Western Reserve University (Cleveland, Ohio), and Iowa State University (Ames, Iowa), among others, exploring the possibilities offered by instructional television. Colleges and universities worked with teachers, instructional designers, graphic artists, educational technologists, and students to find the most effective ways to create and deliver telecourses.

Some schools established, owned, and operated their own television stations in the mid-fifties; examples include the University of Nebraska-Lincoln (KUON) and the University of North Carolina at Chapel Hill (WUNC). Several of these have since developed into highly effective statewide networks. However, colleges and universities that did not own a station or a closed-circuit system got their opportunity to experiment with television courses when the commercial networks became interested in educational television in the late fifties.

WCBS/New York first broadcast the "Sunrise Semester" series in comparative literature in 1957. By 1958, NBC was broadcasting "Atomic Age Physics" on "Continental Classroom" over 150 network stations across the country. Funded in part by a grant from the Ford Foundation, the physics series received high marks from educators for academic quality and the usefulness of the accompanying support materials for students and local teachers. More than three hundred colleges and universities offered "Atomic Age Physics" the first year, and several other courses followed in succeeding years. Unfortunately, the series required heavy subsidy, and NBC dropped it a few seasons later. Nevertheless, educators, programmers and producers learned valuable lessons about telecourses from the experience: a program with high academic standards could be created that would be accepted by teachers and students; a market for such programs existed; and, as always, financial issues needed to be considered. In 1963, CBS made "Sunrise Semester" available to its network stations, and the highly successful program continues today.

Another landmark event for telecourses in the early sixties was the passing of the Federal Educational Television Facilities Act of 1962. This legislation empowered the federal government to fund the building and equipping of public television stations, thereby extending their broadcast reach. In response to the growing interest in telecourses, the Great Plains Regional Instructional Library was created in 1963 by an agency of the KUON-TV/Nebraska ETV Network in affiliation with the University of Nebraska-Lincoln. The library's goal was to serve as a clearinghouse that would acquire, maintain, and lend to schools those programs and series that had continuing educational value. Headquartered in Lincoln, Neb., the library now houses some 2,300 educational programs for elementary, secondary, and higher education and produces the young reader "Reading Rainbow" series for the Public Broadcasting Service.

Probably the biggest advance for educational television occurred with the passage of the Public Broadcasting Act of 1967, which recognized the potential of broadcast television to inform and enlighten (as well as entertain) the public. This legislation authorized the creation of the Corporation for Public Broadcasting (CPB), which was charged with the "responsibility of assisting new stations in getting on the air, establishing one or more systems of interconnection, obtaining grants from federal and other sources, providing funds to support program production, making grants to stations to support local programming and conducting research and training projects."[15]

The Corporation for Public Broadcasting was not a production or networking facility. Instead, another entity, the Public Broadcasting Service (PBS), was created in 1969 to serve as CPB's television network. Its functions were to select, schedule, and distribute programming for the widespread system of PBS-affiliated stations. Through that network, a nationwide system of public television had come into being by the end of the sixties.

In addition to the creation of CPB and PBS, further progress for educational television came with the creation of the British Open University in 1969. Championed by then-Prime Minister Harold Wilson, the Open University was created as an alternative system for achieving a higher education degree. Its courses blended print, video, and radio presentations with campus visits and were designed to appeal to students unable to attend universities full-time or "in residence." To support the needs of its far-flung students, the Open University established several sites throughout Britain where students could go for tests and to meet with tutors. Beginning with an enrollment of 40,000 in 1971, it now enrolls about 64,000 students per year throughout the United Kingdom. The Open University, which has distributed its course materials for use in this country and now has branches in several other countries, helped set the precedent for using television as a key component of basic higher education courses.

In the mid-seventies, colleges and universities began producing their own telecourse series and related support materials to attract broader audiences and extend the reach of their campuses. Miami-Dade Community College (Miami, Fla.), Coastline Community College District (Fountain Valley, Calif.), and Dallas County Community College (Dallas, Texas) were three of the schools most active in this field. Since then, many schools have joined together in regional consortiums that currently produce some of the best telecourse programs available throughout the world.

The eighties witnessed an explosion of alternative instructional delivery systems for public elementary, secondary, and higher education in America. Fueling major research and experimentation during this period was Ambassador Walter Annenberg's establishment in 1981 of the landmark Annenberg/CPB Project, through which the Annenberg School of Communications contracted to provide $10 million a year for fifteen years to CPB. The goal of the project was to expand opportunities for individuals to acquire a quality college education at an affordable cost. To that end, the project supported the development of a collection of telecourses that could be offered to students at more convenient times and places than the traditional classroom hours. It also funded demonstrations of new applications of the telecommunication and information technologies in higher education. The purpose of this funding was to explore improvements in education made possible by advances in technology.[16]

Recently, the federal government has taken a more active role in exploring—and funding—distance education. Perhaps the most ambitious undertaking so far is the federal government's Star Schools Program for elementary and secondary schools. Created by the Omnibus Trade Bill and Competitive Act in 1988, the Star Schools Program was designed to address "critical needs in the rebuilding of our education system to meet domestic and international challenges." In pursuit of this goal, Congress appropriated $33.5 million over a two-year period to ensure United States students "access to basic and advanced courses in mathematics, science, and foreign languages."[17]

The priorities of the Star Schools Program were "to create multistate, organizationally diverse partnerships to write and deliver both core and enrichment curriculum, and to create opportunities for disadvantaged students to receive remote instruction."[18] By insisting on multistate, multi-institutional partnerships, the bill's authors hoped to encourage new alternatives for improving the accessibility of quality education to the nation's remotely located or underserved students. Distance education technology has been the central vehicle for achieving this goal.

The Star Schools Program was authorized as a five-year program with an overall funding limit of $100 million. Four projects were selected for the first two-year grant period, including three satellite-delivered projects and one project based on a combination of computers and telecommunications.

Based on the results of such undertakings, projects utilizing telecommunications technologies such as satellites, cable television, fiber optics, microwave, slow-scan television, microcomputer networks, fax machines, and VCRs have opened up new and exciting opportunities for those interested in distance education.

In the nineties, our challenge will be to build upon the insights and experience gained in the past three decades. These advances have created unprecedented opportunities to tailor education to the needs of the students, rather than having students structure their education around the needs of the institution. ME/U's goal is to ensure that as many students as possible, no matter what their circumstances or location, can take advantage of these opportunities.

With broad-scale ability to become educated comes broad-scale opportunity, economic and otherwise. With recognizable opportunity and broad-scale access to it comes a broad-scale sense of fairness and hope. A sense of fairness and attitude of hope are positive elements in both the individual and national psyches. America needs these elements. They are confidence-builders personally, organizationally and nationally.

---

[1]For detailed discussions of the importance of lifelong learning to our nation's economy and competitive edge, see James Botkin et al, *Global Stakes: The Future of High Technology in America* (Cambridge, Mass.: Ballinger Publishing Company, 1982); William B. Johnston and Arnold H. Packer, *Workforce 2000: Work and Workers for the Twenty-first Century* (Indianapolis, Ind.: Hudson Institute, 1987), pp. xxvi-xxvii and 95-103; Jack E. Bowsher, *Educating America: Lessons Learned in the Nation's Corporations* (New York: John Wiley & Sons, Inc., 1989), pp. 208-220; and *A Nation at Risk: The Full Account* (Cambridge, Mass.: USA Research, for The National Commission on Excellence in Education, 1984).

[2]Ken Dychtwald and Joe Flower, *Age Wave: The Challenges and Opportunities of an Aging America* (Los Angeles: Jeremy P. Tarcher, Inc., 1989), p. 3.

[3]For an analysis of the changing ratio of older students to traditional students and the effects of that change, see Arthur Levine and Associates, *Shaping Higher Education's Future: Demographic Realities and Opportunities, 1990-2000* (San Francisco, Jossey-Bass Publishers, 1989), and current issues of *The Chronicle of Higher Education* (weekly, 1255 23rd St., Washington, DC 20037). Two notable university presidents, Derek Bok of Harvard University and John Silber of Boston University, have also addressed this issue. For their analyses, see Derek Bok, *Higher Learning* (Cambridge, Mass.: Harvard University Press, 1986), pp. 114-128, and John Silber, *Straight Shooting: What's Wrong with America and How to Fix It* (New York: Harper & Row, 1989), pp. 158-170.

[4]Johnston and Packer, *Workforce 2000,* p. 103.

[5]William Bowen and Julie Ann Sosa, *Prospects for Faculty in the Arts and Sciences* (Princeton, N.J.: Princeton University Press, 1989).

[6]The issue of rising costs for college was examined at length in two landmark articles published by one of the nation's leading business publications: Peter Brimelow, "Are we spending too much on education?" *Forbes,* Vol. 138, December 29, 1986, pp. 72-76, and Peter Brimelow, "The untouchables," *Forbes,* Vol. 140, November 30, 1987, pp. 140-146. For current statistics on higher education costs, see the annual *Digest of Education Statistics* (Washington, D.C.: Government Printing Office), or recent issues of *The Chronicle of Higher Education* (weekly, 1255 23rd St., Washington, DC 20037).

[7]Bowsher, *Educating America,* pp. 191-192.

[8]See David T. Kearns and Dennis p. Doyle, *Winning the Brain Race: A Bold Plan to Make Our Schools Competitive* (San Francisco: ICS Press, 1988), pp. 1-14; Jack E. Bowsher, *Educating America: Lessons Learned in the Nation's Corporations* (New York: John Wiley & Sons, Inc., 1989), pp. 13-44; and Marvin Cetron and Thomas O'Toole, *Encounters with the Future: A Forecast of Life Into the 21st Century* (New York: McGraw-Hill, 1982), pp. 253-271. Note also the statement by United Auto Workers economist Daniel Luria, "Resisting automation is probably a lower route to employment than accepting it." (*Encounters with the Future,* p. 267)

[9]Wilson P. Dizard, Jr., *The Coming Information Age: An Overview of Technology, Economics, and Politics, Third Edition* (New York: Longman Inc., 1989), pp. 97-105.

[10]Tom Peters, *Thriving on Chaos; Handbook for a Management Revolution* (New York: Harper & Row, 1987), p. 5.

[11]Johnston and Packer, *Workforce 2000,* pp. xxvi-xxvii.

[12]Johnston and Packer, *Workforce 2000,* pp. 96-97.

[13]United States Congress, Office of Technology Assessment, *Linking for Learning: A New Course for Education,* OTA-SET-430 (Washington, D.C.: U.S. Government Printing Office, November 1989), pp. 27-28.

[14]For a thorough discussion of the history, development and current implementation of educational telecommunications, see *Reaching New Students through New Technologies,* Leslie Noble Purdy, editor (Dubuque, Iowa: Kendall/Hunt Publishing Company for the Coast

Community College, 1983). See also the following articles: Bruce O. Barker et al, "Broadening the definition of distance education in light of the new telecommunications technologies," *The American Journal of Distance Education,* Vol. 3, No. 1, 1989, pp. 20-29; Bernie Ward, "Long-distance learning," *Sky,* April 1989, pp. 53-65; Thomas A. Clark and John R. Verduin, Jr., "Distance education: Its effectiveness and potential use in lifelong learning," *Lifelong Learning,* Vol. 12, No. 4, January 1989, pp. 24-27; and Daniel D. Barron, "Distance education: Removing barriers to knowledge," *School Library Journal,* Vol. 35, November 1989, pp. 28-33.

[15]D. N. Wood and D. G. Wylie, *Educational Telecommunications* (Belmont, Calif.: Wadsworth Publishing Co., 1977), cited in *Reaching New Students through New Technologies,* p. 33.

[16]Annenberg/CPB project statement, 1987.

[17]United States Congress, Senate Committee on Labor and Human Resources, Star Schools Program Assistance Act, Report 100-44, April 21, 1987, p. 1.

[18]*Linking for Learning,* p. 136.

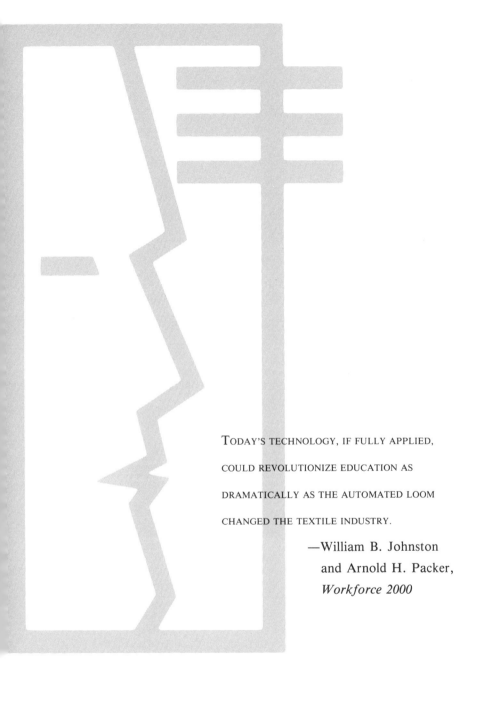

TODAY'S TECHNOLOGY, IF FULLY APPLIED,
COULD REVOLUTIONIZE EDUCATION AS
DRAMATICALLY AS THE AUTOMATED LOOM
CHANGED THE TEXTILE INDUSTRY.

—William B. Johnston
and Arnold H. Packer,
Workforce 2000

MIND EXTENSION UNIVERSITY
The Education Network

MIND EXTENSION UNIVERSITY: THE EDUCATION NETWORK

In November 1987, Mind Extension University was launched as a basic cable television channel designed to meet diverse needs for education, information, and instruction.

Originally, the network's programming focused primarily on for-credit, college-level telecourses in such areas as science, fine arts, English, mathematics, foreign languages, and general business. In addition, a variety of pre-college educational programs and personal enrichment programs were offered. ME/U has since broadened its course offerings to meet the needs not only of college-level students but also of elementary and secondary school students and their teachers.

COLLEGE-LEVEL COURSES

Since ME/U's inception, all credit courses have been led by course instructors from prestigious colleges and universities across the nation. As in traditional on-campus classes, each course requires textbooks, assignments, and exams. Direct or two-way contact with instructors is handled by mail, phone and, in many cases, teleconference. Once a student completes a course, credit is granted by the institution offering the course. These credits may be transferred to other schools.

Recently adding an MBA program, ME/U continues to

expand its course offerings, and is currently exploring the possibility of offering courses from other countries. However, the standard for courses has always been the same: students should receive the best course from the best teacher. Concurrently, the teachers expect the best from their students.

Four factors are considered especially important when selecting those schools and colleges whose courses are carried on ME/U. These are:

- quality of telecourses,
- ability of instructors,
- experience with the theory and practice of televised education, and
- proven support on the part of the institution's leadership for telecourse instruction.

Based on these criteria, eighteen colleges and universities have become part of ME/U programming to date, and more are in the process of joining the network.

Colorado State University in Fort Collins, Colo., was the first school to become part of ME/U. This university has been a leader in the area of telecourse instruction for twenty years and is nationally recognized for its SURGE program, which specializes in video-based courses for business and industry users. Their faculty has a strong commitment to televised instruction, a commitment that is echoed by the administration through additional salary and graduate student support. The university's College of Business, a twenty-year leader in video-based, graduate business education, is now offering through ME/U the first American Assembly of Collegiate Schools of Business-accredited MBA by satellite broadcast and cable delivery.

ELEMENTARY AND SECONDARY SCHOOL COURSES

A broad range of courses to meet the educational needs of the nation's elementary and secondary schools is provided by ME/U through a cooperative agreement with the TI-IN Network. TI-IN Network is a Texas-based provider of live, interactive television instruction.[1]

These courses are delivered to schools each day as part of ME/U's regular educational programming. This programming currently encompasses 21 high school credit classes in science, the humanities, foreign languages, and math. The courses include subjects that would be impossible for many small, economically disadvantaged, or geographically remote schools to provide—for example, marine science, trigonometry, Japanese, French, and staff development programming. Student enrichment programs tailored to specific grade levels (elementary through high school) supplement the for-credit courses.

HOW MIND EXTENSION UNIVERSITY WORKS

Mind Extension University courses are transmitted by satellite to cable television systems, then by cable into students' homes or businesses as well as to libraries and school classrooms.

COLLEGE-LEVEL COURSES

Usually students use a videocassette recorder to tape the class, then replay it at their convenience. This enables students to fit coursework into their own schedules and gives them the opportunity to review classes in order to more fully understand the topic's concepts or the instructor's points. Students who miss a lesson can call the ME/U Student Support Center, and a representative will immediately send a replacement tape so that there is little interruption in the continuity of the course.

Each month, a program schedule listing the course offerings for that period is sent to students and others who have indicated an interest in the telecourses. (Research indicates that most ME/U students "preview" or watch a course at least once before enrolling in it.) Registered students receive a syllabus that lists an entire semester's schedule of their courses. In addition, the course catalog indicates what dates a course will be offered, and gives a description of the course content, credit, and cost. Courses generally begin in September, January, and May, similar to the schedule a student would expect from a traditional semester structure.

Getting started. Students who sign up for college-level courses receive a copy of the *Telecourse Student Survival Handbook* for the appropriate course. The handbook explains administrative procedures, course requirements, assignment and exam procedures, grades, and other relevant information, and includes a broadcast schedule with lesson numbers, dates and times. The purpose of this material is to streamline the administrative process as much as possible so that the student's efforts go into studying and learning rather than into filling out forms and standing in lines.

Students also receive a study guide and a syllabus or letter from the instructor outlining the details of the course and covering information such as assignments and exams. If the course calls for a proctored exam (for example, all of the MBA classes require proctored exams, wherein the proctor, or individual administering the exam, must sign and have notarized a proctor statement), this information will also be included.

Attending college-level classes. Once the preliminaries are taken care of, students are ready to start "attending class" in their homes or offices. Classes are televised weekly. As mentioned, students usually videotape the programs and then watch them at a convenient, but regular, time each week. Most ME/U students stress that consistency of personal scheduling is important to maintain the continuity of the course and to stay on top of assignments.

Depending on the originating school's schedule, courses run for a quarter or a semester, similar to on-campus classes. Although students are encouraged to complete the courses within the regular quarter or semester schedule, it is understood that ME/U students frequently face personal and professional disruptions to their studies. Consequently, course extensions may be arranged if necessary. As with any questions regarding scheduling, classwork, or related concerns, ME/U representatives at the Student Support Center will work with students to help resolve course completion problems.

ELEMENTARY AND SECONDARY SCHOOL COURSES

Any viewer interested in ME/U programming at the elementary or secondary school level can call a toll-free number and speak with a Student Support Center representative for information about the courses. Elementary and secondary schools wishing to use the courses to augment their curriculum with classroom-delivered telecourses available on the network may call for registration information and materials.

Interested callers may request a course catalog that describes subscriber services, staff development programs, special programs, student enrichment programs, and direct student instruction courses. The catalog includes the annual programming calendar and information on all policies and procedures. Additionally, teachers are encouraged to call with questions they may have. Because staff members work regularly with both teachers and school districts across the country, questions can be handled quickly and knowledgeably.

STUDENT SUPPORT SERVICES

A Student Support Center is staffed at ME/U's head-quarters in Englewood, Colo., to support the ME/U-affiliated colleges and universities and the administrative needs of ME/U students. Through the center, ME/U representatives assist students with enrollment (among other things), bill them for tuition and fees, mail textbooks and support materials, and arrange exams. Representatives also refer students to local schools when appropriate and provide information regarding transfer of credits.

Registered students are also provided with "missed lesson" videotape rentals. Instructor contact is maintained through a phone mail system, and, for some classes, through a computer bulletin board arrangement that allows students to discuss questions and concerns with both instructors and other students, and through periodic teleconferences with professors to review important course topics.

THE ME/U PROCESS

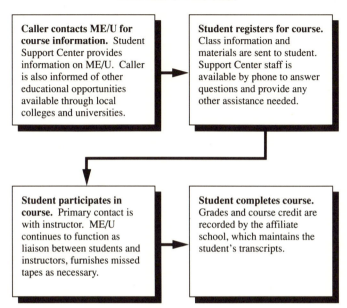

Caller contacts ME/U for course information. Student Support Center provides information on ME/U. Caller is also informed of other educational opportunities available through local colleges and universities.

Student registers for course. Class information and materials are sent to student. Support Center staff is available by phone to answer questions and provide any other assistance needed.

Student participates in course. Primary contact is with instructor. ME/U continues to function as liaison between students and instructors, furnishes missed tapes as necessary.

Student completes course. Grades and course credit are recorded by the affiliate school, which maintains the student's transcripts.

THE HOME/OFFICE CLASSROOM

One of the most exciting aspects of ME/U is that many of its students are eager to use advanced communications technologies. Reflecting the communications advances currently available to distance education, ME/U's at-home students may have in their home classrooms:

- a television connected to a cable or a satellite receive dish, either of which enables the television to receive a channel devoted entirely to education;
- a VCR, connected to the television, that allows students to record the programming required for their course(s); and
- a telephone line that enables them to communicate with other students or their instructors through a voice mail system on a toll-free number.

In a growing number of at-home ME/U classrooms, students also have computers that can connect them with their

classmates and instructor through a modem (a device that con-
nects a computer with the telephone lines for communication
purposes), an electronic bulletin-board, and a telephone
number. It is expected that soon home fax machines may
become as common as VCRs (and much less expensive), thereby
giving students the ability to electronically send print material
to their classmates and instructors. While greatly enhancing
the delivery of ME/U course content, these tools also shorten
the communication distance between instructor and student,
as well as between and among students.

EDUCATIONAL ENRICHMENT PROGRAMS

As part of its commitment to education, ME/U also tele-
casts educational enrichment and pre-college programs. This
programming is designed to further an important ME/U goal,
which is to become an educational channel that mirrors a complete educational institution. In addition to academic classes,
students might receive self-improvement and recreational
programming such as campus theater productions, lecture
series, public debates, a tour of a bookstore with the latest and
best titles, library programs, and other enrichment activities.

Mind Extension University is committed to enabling its
students not only to see these activities on television but,
through the innovative use of advances in communications
technology, to *participate* in them in a truly interactive way.
The enabling technology is close enough at hand to start plan-
ning its imaginative and effective use.

COSTS

The increasing cost of higher education affects all Americans intending to pursue a degree or to send a child through
college. As noted earlier, one of the most pressing concerns
regarding higher education is the increase in the costs of attending college. Tuition costs for ME/U reflect those of its participating schools and fall midway between most public and

moderately priced private institutions. Tables 1 and 2 detail
the cost relationships.

TABLE 1

TWO-YEAR COLLEGES
1989–90 AVERAGE COSTS PER SEMESTER (12 CREDITS)

Costs	Public	Private	ME/U
Tuition and fees*	$842 (1992)	$4713	$1176
Room and board	†	3258	Existing costs at home
Books and supplies	438	424	450
Transportation	†	423	Existing costs at home
Personal	†	832	Existing costs at home
Total	†	$9650	$1626 (plus costs at home)

*Non-resident tuition and fees given in parentheses
†Insufficient data
Source: based on figures cited in *The Chronicle of Higher Education,*
August 16, 1989

TABLE 2

FOUR-YEAR COLLEGES
1989–90 AVERAGE COSTS PER SEMESTER (12 CREDITS)

Costs	Public	Private	ME/U
Tuition and fees*	$1694 (2684)	$8737	$2136
Room and board	3039	3898	Existing costs at home
Books and supplies	454	459	450
Transportation	442	414	Existing costs at home
Personal	1042	818	Existing costs at home
Total	$6671 (7661)	$14,326	$2586 (plus costs at home)

*Non-state resident tuition and fees given in parentheses
Source: based on figures cited in *The Chronicle of Higher Education,*
August 16, 1989

The financial advantage ME/U students have over their on-campus counterparts is that they pay only for their education, not for school-related transportation, housing, athletic or health fees, or various other costs incurred in living away from home (see Table 3). In addition, and perhaps equally important, ME/U students realize a substantial time savings. While the rigors of success in a course are the same, ME/U students don't have to spend time away from their jobs or families as do those who attend classes on campus.

TABLE 3

COMPARISON OF COSTS, FINANCIAL AND PERSONAL,
AMONG COLLEGE ALTERNATIVES

Costs	On Campus	Commuter	ME/U
Tuition	Yes	Yes	Yes
Fees (student, athletic, library, other)	Yes	Yes	No
Room and board	Yes	No	No
Transportation	Yes	Yes	No
Personal	Yes	Yes	Yes
Books	Yes	Yes	Yes
Time away from job and family	Yes	Yes	No

LOOKING FORWARD

Even though ME/U is often referred to as "the degree channel," its student body, in a broad sense, also includes millions of learners not formally pursuing a degree. Programming from ME/U engages the minds of these individuals simply because they have an interest in the political process, in history, in mathematics, in languages, in library information science, in the planet Earth, in the nature of the universe, in thermodynamics, in computer literacy, in literature, in knowing how to write more effectively, in the general education development (GED) program, or in any of the long list of subjects offered through ME/U.

The channel is dedicated to equality of educational opportunity for everyone, regardless of his or her station in life or depth of interest in the formal educational process. The channel's philosophy is that if you watch you learn, and learning is positive. It is mind engaging; it is the antithesis of being a "couch potato."

American higher education has been a leader in the challenge to produce an informed electorate, a productive work force, and a nation prepared to adapt to change. However, changing societal and economic demands are forcing us to move beyond traditional responses.

We must embrace innovative solutions. In ME/U's case, this entails fusing the strengths of our educators' expertise and leadership with technological advances. In order to improve and enhance its service, ME/U will rely on a time-honored strategy of American business: it will learn in the marketplace from its clients, the students of ME/U, and from its partners, traditional educators.

---

[1]As the use of telecourses and other video-based programs has grown, so too have the number and type of groups providing programming alternatives. Some, like Pacific Mountain Network, function as a clearinghouse of information and programs for a network of member educational institutions. Others, such as Canada-based TV Ontario, produce their own high-quality programs and sell them to educational institutions throughout the world.

Several of the largest providers are nonprofit consortiums comprising member states' education agencies and educational television authorities. Two highly successful examples of this type of programming provider are the twelve-state Satellite Telecommunications Educational Programming Network (STEP) based in Washington state and the nineteen-state Satellite Educational Resources Consortium (SERC) headquartered in Columbia, South Carolina. Both have received Star Schools Program funding from the federal government.

Commercial program providers have stepped forward to offer other programming alternatives. These alternatives are informative and useful as supplements to in-class instruction but typically do not carry secondary school or university credit. A recent, controversial entry into this arena is Whittle Communications' satellite-delivered Channel One, a news-based program for high schools that has engendered much interest because advertising is included in its tele-casts. Although several state boards of education have prohibited their schools from signing up with Channel One, it nevertheless provides another option for educators looking for new ways to provide infor-mation to their students.

A less controversial alternative is provided by cable television operators, who have joined together to provide schools with newscasts from CNN as well as current events and other informative program-ming from such channels as C-SPAN, Discovery, Arts & Entertain-ment, Disney, and others. The cable industry has coordinated its efforts under the name of Cable in the Classroom. Its offerings to date are without commercials, and ME/U has contributed its not-for-credit Global Library Project programming to this effort.

It should also be noted that the cable industry is rapidly provid-ing free cable connections to most of the nation's schools. The impact of this undertaking could prove to be dramatic if the connections are appropriately utilized.

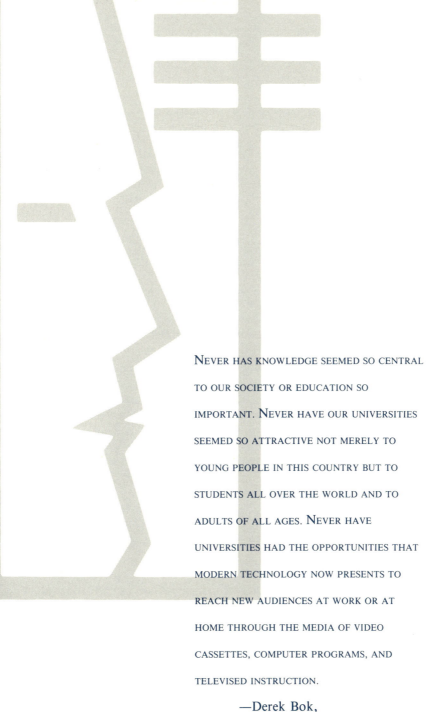

NEVER HAS KNOWLEDGE SEEMED SO CENTRAL TO OUR SOCIETY OR EDUCATION SO IMPORTANT. NEVER HAVE OUR UNIVERSITIES SEEMED SO ATTRACTIVE NOT MERELY TO YOUNG PEOPLE IN THIS COUNTRY BUT TO STUDENTS ALL OVER THE WORLD AND TO ADULTS OF ALL AGES. NEVER HAVE UNIVERSITIES HAD THE OPPORTUNITIES THAT MODERN TECHNOLOGY NOW PRESENTS TO REACH NEW AUDIENCES AT WORK OR AT HOME THROUGH THE MEDIA OF VIDEO CASSETTES, COMPUTER PROGRAMS, AND TELEVISED INSTRUCTION.

—Derek Bok,
President, Harvard University,
Higher Learning

MIND EXTENSION UNIVERSITY
The Education Network™

UNLIMITED ACCESS

For centuries, colleges and universities have expected students to deliver themselves to education. Large-scale delivery of education to students is a substantial change in approach: it places the needs of the students, rather than those of the faculty, at the center of the education equation.

The ability to respond to students' needs is one of the key elements that makes ME/U so useful: it is "student-friendly," stressing convenience of coursework viewing and accessibility of instructors. As cable subscribers, ME/U students also create pressure in the marketplace to serve them well, because ME/U must answer to cable operators whose prerogative it is to carry or not carry the channel on local cable systems.

The flexibility of taking classes through ME/U is manifested in a number of ways. Students whose jobs require travel can record lessons for viewing later. As mentioned earlier, students who miss a session can receive a videotape of the missed program. Students who must relocate can often continue their coursework with little, if any, disruption in their degree program if ME/U is available at their new location.

At the elementary through secondary school level, the network allows parents who are at home during the day and whose cable systems carry ME/U to see how their children are doing in class. By watching the class presentation and becoming familiar with class materials and homework requirements, parents are able to more fully support their children's academic efforts. This kind of participation enables parents to play an important role in the educational equation.

The variety of students served by ME/U reflects the diversity of programming that marks ME/U's approach to education. At the beginning, the main focus was college-level courses, at the associate's, bachelor's, and master's level, in a variety of curriculum areas. However, as the network has continued to evolve, the focus has broadened to include programs aimed at students needing to complete their high school studies, improve their English, mathematics, science, or language skills, or develop a better understanding of the world around them. The concept underlying ME/U's programming is not just to provide an opportunity to complete high school requirements or college credits. It is also to create excitement about education and to facilitate lifelong learning in a constantly changing society.

The diversity of ME/U courses makes them valuable to a wide range of age and interest groups. In fact, any cable television system that carries the ME/U channel or any television set connected to a satellite receive dish can deliver education to students, either individually or in groups.

FULL- OR PART-TIME EMPLOYEES

Many nontraditional students must support themselves and their families while pursuing a college education. These students need flexible scheduling that will enable them to undertake college coursework without disrupting their job responsibilities.

Night classes or print-based correspondence courses have often been the only option available to this type of student. Night classes, however, frequently necessitate child care arrangements and being out late at night. Mind Extension University provides an alternative means of pursuing a diploma or college degree, an alternative that offers convenience, flexible scheduling, and the comfort of one's own home.

HOMEBOUND PARENTS

Homebound parents are individuals who are currently stay-ing at home to raise young children. Their schedules are primarily geared to the needs and activities of their children.

Many of these parents, however, view their at-home child-rearing time as part of an overall family/career approach that entails spending several years at home with young ones and then re-entering the job market. Mind Extension University offers these individuals an opportunity to upgrade their educa-tional achievements and professional skills while they are at home. Coursework and studies can be arranged around the children's daily routines, avoiding the need for child care and the inevitable scheduling conflicts that would result from trying to attend on-campus classes.

PHYSICALLY CHALLENGED MEN AND WOMEN

For America's physically challenged men and women, a key component of living a productive life is equality of access: access to public transportation and buildings, access to job opportunities, access to education. However, for many wheel-chair-bound and other physically challenged students, such access is an impossibility.

Mind Extension University offers a practical means of achieving barrier-free access to education. Because learning takes place in the student's home, ME/U students are able to attend classes and study in an environment tailored to their particular needs. As a society, we have a long way to go before we can offer a truly barrier-free environment, but ME/U represents a positive first step for many physically challenged students.

SHIFT WORKERS

Like other students who are employed part-time or full-time, shift workers must dovetail their college coursework with the scheduling demands of their jobs. Shift workers, however, often have to cope with the added disadvantage of schedules that change frequently or require unusual amounts of time per shift. For example, firefighters may work four days and have three days off during one week, then alternate the schedule the following week.

This type of work schedule makes attending most on-campus classes impossible. The flexible scheduling provided by ME/U classes, however, offers an effective means for combining shift work with pursuit of continuing education or a college degree.

GEOGRAPHICALLY REMOTE INDIVIDUALS

Americans living in geographically remote locations are often unable to travel the distance to the nearest college campus, and that campus may not offer the curriculum they need. Individuals in these situations are unable to pursue further education in order to change occupations or to enhance their current job skills. As the number of family farms continues to decrease, for example, more and more rural workers need to explore other industries and job options. Distance education can offer them an opportunity to complete their education or to upgrade their skills as they contemplate such a transition.

MILITARY PERSONNEL

One of the benefits of a military career is that the government helps to pay for its employees' educations. The drawback, however, is that military personnel are often moved about so frequently that it becomes impossible for them to complete many college-level courses, let alone a degree program.

Mind Extension University is able to overcome the difficulties caused by relocation because it is available by cable or satellite throughout the United States and at various overseas locations. Thus, it enables military personnel to earn college degrees, upgrade their rank, or simply pursue intellectual interests.

Individuals who have spent their professional lives in the military but are contemplating a second career upon completion of their service can use ME/U to get a head start toward their goals. The education available through ME/U can help them prepare to compete in the work environment they have chosen.

SENIORS

In *The Three Boxes of Life,* author Richard Bolles observes that traditionally we have organized our lives according to three periods or "boxes": getting an education, going to work and earning a living, and living in retirement. Arguing that this "boxed-in" approach to life is at best limiting and at worst damaging, Bolles calls instead for a lifelong flow that incorporates all three elements concurrently to achieve a balanced, dynamic and productive life.

Today's seniors are breaking out of the retirement box with energy and enthusiasm, and they're finding lifelong learning to be one of their most powerful allies. In 1987, one in ten college students was over 50. The success of the Elderhostel program, a nationally offered, campus-based program of courses for seniors, clearly demonstrates the increasing interest of seniors in lifelong learning. According to Annette Buchanan, American Association of Retired Persons (AARP) program specialist for consumer affairs,

> [Elderhostel] started in 1975 with only 200 students enrolled at 5 colleges in New Hampshire. In 1987, just 12 years later, Elderhostel enrolled 150,000 students in 850 colleges in the U.S., as well as 200 institutions overseas located in 37 countries. Elderhostel has never done any marketing or paid for an advertisement. Yet, this year alone, Elderhostel had more than 150,000 unsolicited requests for catalogs beyond the normal mailing list sent to former attendees. According to Elderhostel president, Bill Berkeley, they cannot keep abreast with the demand and cannot find sufficient space for new Elderhostel programs.[2]

Senior students are looking for personal enrichment, intellectual challenge, and increasingly, upgrading of professional skills. Yet, according to Buchanan, they also want "classes during the day with easy accessibility, since walking long distances can be difficult," and because parking problems often become yet another deterrent to class attendance on campus.[3] The convenience, comfort, and safety of learning in their own homes offers many seniors educational opportunities they might otherwise miss.

PRISON INMATES

Another potential user group is prison inmates. As noted by Bruce Wolford in his chapter on correctional facilities in *The Handbook of Adult and Continuing Education,* "In many correctional institutions, educators provide one of the few positive change-oriented programs available to inmates."[4] Wolford also notes that our prisons include "a disproportionate number of unemployed, undereducated, and learning handicapped individuals," that more than 80 percent of these prisoners did not complete high school, and that "60 to 80 percent have been classified as functionally illiterate."[5]

This is a disaster both for the prisoners who are unable to break out of their destructive lifestyles and for our society, which bears the scars of their ongoing crimes. Education is one of the tools that can check this downward spiral. Yet for obvious reasons, few inmates have the opportunity to attend classes.

Many prisoners know firsthand the difficulties they will confront in attempting to rejoin society if they have not developed the skills necessary to compete in the work force. Consequently, although prison inmates frequently need substantial remedial education (ME/U's GED coursework can be especially helpful for prisoners who never completed high school), those who take advantage of educational opportunities are usually quite motivated and committed to completing their programs.

Although changing criminal behavior patterns is one of society's most perplexing challenges, the experts identify educational opportunities as a key component in prison reform. Learning creates understanding, opportunity and hope; these displace anger.

COLLEGES AND UNIVERSITIES

The escalating costs of hiring professors in certain fields[6] may seriously impair the ability of all but major institutions to offer students a well-rounded curriculum. Courses offered through ME/U can help provide a solution to this growing problem. Colleges and universities can use ME/U's satellite-delivered programming as on-campus stand-alone courses or as a component of the institution's division of continuing education. In the former instance, the school supplies its own catalog number and instructor and offers its own credit. In "wrap-around" courses, instructors begin and conclude the class with their own material, wrapping it around the televised material that forms the core of the course. In the latter instance, ME/U programming is usually offered through the school's division of continuing education as a telecourse for individuals in the local community, who, because of scheduling or logistics conflicts, would otherwise be unable to attend the school's on-campus classes.

With either method ME/U saves the institution's instructors time and effort in preparation and allows the instructors to see how colleagues cover the course material. Institutions may also find that offering ME/U programming through the division of continuing education enables them to enroll more students.

ELEMENTARY AND SECONDARY SCHOOLS

Elementary and secondary schools, especially those constrained by geographic isolation, funding limitations, or teacher shortages, are one of ME/U's largest constituencies. ME/U programming enables these schools to:
- provide access to courses for which they have no teachers;
- offer graduate courses and in-service programs for teachers, administrators, school librarians, and school support staff;
- enhance or broaden the curriculum they are already delivering to their students; and
- offer academically advanced students a head start on college coursework (many entry-level college courses have study guides and textbooks designed for high school use).

In the future, ME/U plans to offer schools the opportunity to participate in innovative, single-event programs. As communications advances have opened up new interactive possibilities, single-event programs have become a popular way to introduce students to the excitement of exploration and discovery, be it in the sciences, literature, the arts, or simply the exchange of ideas. Although single-event programs may originate from many different sources (research institutes, museums, national forums, professional associations, art galleries, and national libraries are but a few), they have in common the goal of providing opportunities for students to participate in specialized learning experiences or events that would otherwise be unavailable to them.[7]

BUSINESS AND INDUSTRY

Business and industry comprise another constituency for ME/U's educational programming. America's blue-collar work force is currently made up of some 32 million men and women. Many of these individuals lack an adequate pre-college education and may need to take GED courses, preferably at the work site. Moreover, although in the past a high school education was sufficient to enable blue-collar workers to perform their jobs successfully, today a bachelor's degree is more frequently necessary to compete in the labor market. Additionally, a growing number of professions require a master's degree either to start in the profession or to remain in it. Many companies insist that their employees complete such degrees within two or three years of employment or face termination.

Although the demand for further education for American workers has increased radically over the past decade, there has not been a similar increase in educational alternatives for this group. Many full-time workers do not have the option to attend traditionally scheduled, on-campus classes; as already noted, shift workers in particular find it difficult to continue their education in any traditional way.

For students who need to continue working while completing their high school education, upgrading their skills, or preparing for a career change, ME/U offers a way to pursue their education while maintaining their employment.

SPECIALIZED DEGREE PROGRAMS

COMPLETION PROGRAM

Many of the potential students just described may have started higher education programs but for various reasons were unable to continue them. To meet the needs of these students, ME/U delivers an associate degree and a bachelors' completion degree with a management focus.

The associate's degree is based on a general curriculum so that courses will easily transfer into the bachelor's degree programs of other colleges and universities.

The bachelor's completion program, designed for adult students who wish to sharpen existing management skills or learn new ones, allows students to supplement its management focus with a secondary concentration that supports their career goals. The degree's business curriculum focuses on current issues (including global perspectives), ethical and legal considerations, practical problem solving, and critical thinking.

Structured for maximum flexibility, the program accepts credit for work experience as well as a wide variety of school transfer credits, so that students from diverse academic backgrounds need not lose credit for the coursework they have already completed.

MASTER'S IN LIBRARY AND INFORMATION SCIENCE

Library and information science is an exciting component of ME/U programming. With existing library and information science courses from the University of South Carolina forming the basis of this ME/U degree program, additional course work is being developed.

Mind Extension University is working with a consortium of several institutions that have graduate-level library and information science programs to develop a master's degree curriculum comprising courses drawn from the participating schools. The goals of the consortium are to (1) develop a library science master's program accessible to students who cannot attend on-campus classes, and (2) allow consortium schools an opportunity to offer courses to their on-campus students that the individual schools might not otherwise be able to provide.

Undertaken with the support and advisement of the American Library Association, this consortium is breaking ground in the innovative use of teaching technology. Few graduate programs, library science or otherwise, have the faculty and resources to offer all the courses that might be desirable in a given discipline. Combined with a consortium approach, however, ME/U's telecourse technology enables schools to share faculty with one another, expanding the reach and services of each institution.

Consortium members will agree on a curriculum and on which institutional members will teach each course. Participants will also agree to transfer credits from other member institutions. This inter-institutional cooperation will allow students to benefit from the broad-based strengths of several schools rather than being restricted to the offerings of just one. Students enrolled in an existing on-campus program will be able to take consortium courses in addition to their regular classes; students in remote locations will be able to complete all coursework through the ME/U programming.

The consortium model for graduate education is also being adapted for use in a master's level teacher-education program. The focus here will be twofold: (1) to maximize the effective use of each institution's graduate program resources, and (2) to assist in preparing teachers to meet the Professional Teaching Standards, a teacher-certification method that may become a requirement for teaching in the near future.

MASTER'S LEVEL TEACHER EDUCATION

The current move toward new teacher-certification rules will have a tremendous impact on existing teachers as well as on future professionals. Some states are abolishing the undergraduate education major at their colleges and universities and instead are requiring prospective teachers to focus on the subjects they will one day teach. The new rules require teachers to hold a master's degree to receive permanent certification.

This will likely cause an increasing demand for telecourses as attempts are made to get quality information to a large, dispersed audience in a reasonably short period of time. In the meantime, ME/U is working with Penn State and other institutions to offer high-quality in-service training for the nation's teachers and other education staff.

MASTER'S IN BUSINESS ADMINISTRATION

To date, the most sought-after coursework among ME/U students and corporate clients has been graduate-level business classes. In response to this need, ME/U now carries the coursework for the Master's of Business Administration from Colorado State University. The degree coursework carried on the ME/U cable channel is also available by satellite reception and by videotape. In addition to the MBA coursework, ME/U will also offer business school short courses from Colorado State.

The first and only MBA degree program delivered nationally on cable television and by satellite broadcast, Colorado State's MBA program is accredited by the American Assembly of Collegiate Schools of Business (AACSB). (Of the 750 business degree programs currently available in the United States, only 266 have met AACSB accreditation standards.) Colorado State's College of Business, which has been providing business education for more than 25 years, has a faculty that combines excellent academic credentials with strong business experience. More than 90 percent of the regular business faculty hold doctoral degrees, and more than 50 percent have had significant business experience with major corporations.

Graduate courses are scheduled throughout the year, and the MBA degree may be completed through ME/U in as few as three years. As with other ME/U degree programs, students enroll in courses through ME/U and receive credit from the sponsoring institution, in this case Colorado State.

The MBA program focuses on preparation for a broad-based, general management career and is designed primarily, but not exclusively, for students with nonbusiness undergraduate degrees. Theoretical approaches are blended with the practical application of decision-making in today's business world. The program offers a wide range of courses such as finance, marketing, organizational structure, and information systems.

This degree, with its flexible scheduling and ability to address the student's needs, will be especially useful to lower level managers who want to upgrade their professional options without disrupting their employment schedules, to individuals (such as career military personnel) who would like to augment their technical degrees with a broader, management-oriented graduate degree but live in geographically remote areas or face relocation, and to others simply trying to keep their professional skills current with changes in the employment marketplace.

To qualify for the MBA degree, students must have the equivalent of a "common body of knowledge" in business and administration as defined by the AACSB. This body of knowledge, which can be acquired either at the undergraduate or graduate level, includes satisfactory work in basic economics, mathematics and statistics, accounting, finance, management and human resources, marketing, production and operations management, computer-based information systems, and business policy. The 30 credit hours that comprise the Common Body of Knowledge Program can be taken from Colorado State or ME/U or can be transferred from another accredited college.

Once students have completed a series of courses designed to bring them to this common point of preparation and have been accepted into the Colorado State graduate program, they are then ready to begin the College of Business's Professional Graduate Program. Of the 33 credit hours that make up the Professional Graduate Program, at least 27 must be from Colorado State.

The program draws on Colorado State's twenty years of experience with televised instruction to offer course material that is both innovative and practical. Tuition for this degree program, based on 33 credit hours, falls midway between that of other public and private college and university MBA programs (see Table 4).

TABLE 4

MBA PROGRAMS
1989–90 AVERAGE COSTS PER SEMESTER (12 CREDITS)

Costs	Public	Private	ME/U
Tuition and fees*	$1564 (2973)	$5202	$3600
Room and board	2092	2092	Existing costs at home
Books and supplies	331	450	425
Transportation	400	400	Existing costs at home
Personal	1913	1913	Existing costs at home
Total	$6300 (7709)*	$10,057	$4025 (plus costs at home)

*Non-resident tuition and fees given in parentheses.
Source: based on figures cited in *Official Guide to MBA Programs, 1988–89 Edition,* Educational Testing Service; transportation figures based on average costs cited in higher education publications

When room and board, transportation, and personal costs are added in, the savings realized by ME/U students are substantial.

[1]Richard N. Bolles, *The Three Boxes of Life, And How to Get Out of Them* (Berkeley, Calif.: Ten Speed Press, 1978).

[2]Annette Buchanan, "An emerging new group on the campus," *Lifelong Learning,* Vol. 11, No. 5, February 1988, pp. 4-6.

[3]Buchanan, "An emerging new group on the campus," p. 4.

[4]Bruce I. Wolfold, "Correctional Facilities," in *The Handbook of Adult and Continuing Education,* Sharon B. Merriam and Phyllis M. Cunningham, editors (San Francisco, Calif.: Jossey-Bass Publishers, 1989), p. 357.

[5]Wolford, "Correctional Facilities," pp. 356-7.

[6]For a sobering overview of the rising costs of hiring faculty, see Charles J. Sykes, *ProfScam: Professors and the Demise of Higher Education* (Washington, DC: Regnery Gateway, 1988).

[7]The highly successful JASON Project provides an outstanding example of the possibilities offered by interactive, single-event programs.

Masterminded in 1988 by Dr. Robert Ballard, marine geologist at the Woods Hole Oceanographic Institute and discoverer of the Titanic, the JASON Project allowed students to experience "close up" the exhilarating process of scientific exploration and discovery.

Ballard's idea was to use telecommunications to enable students from all over the country to watch and participate as JASON, the remote-controlled robot vessel, explored the floor of the Mediterranean Sea. As JASON explored, live video images were sent by its undersea cameras to the research ship, where Ballard and other scientists at the ship's command center explained the nature and history of JASON's archeological and oceanographic finds. The undersea images and accompanying commentary were then telecommunicated to some 250,000 eager fourth- through twelfth-grade science students gathered at twelve American and Canadian science museums. In addition to receiving the video images, students were able to view the scientists as they evaluated the marine environment JASON was exploring and to participate in question-and-answer sessions with Ballard and the ship's crew.

The JASON Project was a collaborative effort involving, among others, the Woods Hole Oceanographic Institute, Electronic Data Systems, the Quest Group, Ltd., Turner Broadcasting, the National Geographic Society, the National Science Foundation, the National Science Teachers Association, and the National Council for Social Studies.

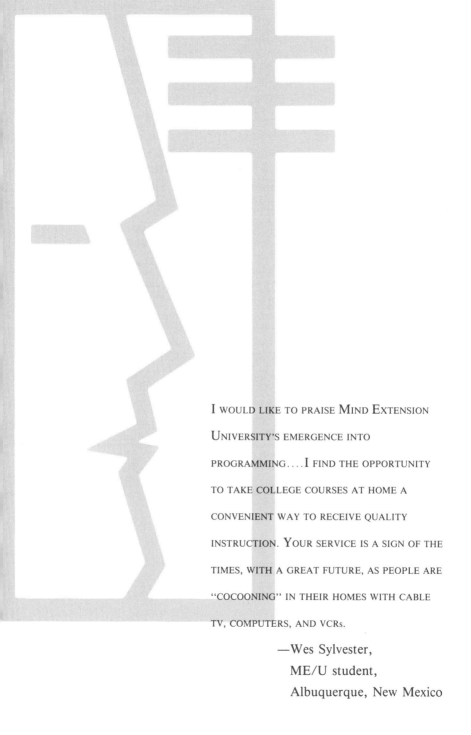

I WOULD LIKE TO PRAISE MIND EXTENSION
UNIVERSITY'S EMERGENCE INTO
PROGRAMMING....I FIND THE OPPORTUNITY
TO TAKE COLLEGE COURSES AT HOME A
CONVENIENT WAY TO RECEIVE QUALITY
INSTRUCTION. YOUR SERVICE IS A SIGN OF THE
TIMES, WITH A GREAT FUTURE, AS PEOPLE ARE
"COCOONING" IN THEIR HOMES WITH CABLE
TV, COMPUTERS, AND VCRs.

—Wes Sylvester,
ME/U student,
Albuquerque, New Mexico

MIND EXTENSION UNIVERSITY
The Education Network™

MIND EXTENSION UNIVERSITY HIGHER EDUCATION STUDENTS

Students enrolled in Mind Extension University courses represent diverse backgrounds, a broad range of ages, and widely varied goals. Many are striving to enhance their career opportunities or to attain other personal and professional objectives. Some audit courses simply out of curiosity or a commitment to lifelong learning. All, however, cite ME/U's ability to bring the classroom to the student as central to pursuit of their studies. The following profiles of eight ME/U students illustrate the advantages ME/U offers individuals in a variety of circumstances.

Steve Zullo, full-time teacher
Libertyville, Illinois

Many individuals who have full-time jobs in demanding occupations credit ME/U's flexible scheduling with enabling them to pursue professional certification. Such was the case for school psychologist Steve Zullo.

Along with two colleagues who teach high school students with behavioral disorders, Zullo took three education classes during the summer of 1988 to continue his certification. Married and the father of two children, 41-year-old Zullo noted that between teaching and coaching, he and his two friends were extremely busy and that "cable TV allowed us to videotape the class and then view it when we had the time. This way we could also do the homework as time permitted. I could work on the classes at night when my children were busy. Or sometimes when everyone else was in bed asleep, I turned on the videotape and started working on my homework."

Zullo and his friends, Robert Mueller and Howard Litwin, teach in Des Plaines, Ill. Because Zullo's local cable company carries ME/U programming, he was the resource for the group. "The others can't get ME/U where they live, so I videotaped the courses on my recorder, did my assignments on Monday, and passed the tape on to Bob or Howard. Then they passed it on to the other guy."

When they enrolled, the three men were assigned a Colorado State University professor with whom they were in regular contact. They sent assignments in weekly and consulted with their professor by telephone or mail. On completion of their courses, they received credit from Colorado State.

Robin Pappas, home-bound parent
Lodi, Ohio

Few people experience a more demanding full-time occupation than stay-at-home parents of small children. Yet while raising their children, many parents want to continue their education. For some, this phase of their lives can offer a chance to upgrade or reinforce important professional skills while they take time off from their careers to care for their children. For many, it can be an opportunity to catch up on courses they never had a chance to take during their college years. For others, it may be an opportunity to begin an undergraduate degree for the first time, as it was for Robin Pappas.

An Ohio mother of three small children, Pappas had never had the opportunity to attend college. Once she became a mother, her family responsibilities and busy lifestyle made attending on-campus classes nearly impossible for her. Pappas faced an urgent problem, however: with no college background or work experience in accounting, she needed training that would enable her to manage the family business.

In the spring of 1988, in the privacy of her living room, Robin Pappas went back to school for the first time in twenty years. Mind Extension University's "Accounting I," offered by the University of New Mexico, provided the introductory accounting coursework she had been looking for. "I wanted to take some business courses so I could help my husband in his business. He drives a semi-trailer truck and also has a home picnic table business and needed me to handle the bookkeeping for both," explained Pappas. After completing the accounting coursework, she set up and continues to maintain official ledgers for both businesses. Pappas subsequently enrolled in the University of Minnesota's "Introduction to Technical and Business Communications" course and in Oxnard College's marketing course. She is currently enrolled in "Introduction to Geology" offered by Colorado State.

With the nearest college twenty miles away and a husband who travels, Pappas found that ME/U's flexibility was the key to her success. "For a mother with small children, this is ideal," she noted. "I tape the classes on my VCR and set aside an hour from seven to eight A.M. every day, when I have quiet time to study. I like the independent study because it lets me fit the classes into my schedule. The advice I would give to others is to stay motivated and discipline yourself to set aside time each day for studying."

Martin Shepard, U.S. Marine
Alexandria, Virginia

Staying motivated and ME/U's scheduling flexibility were what finally enabled Martin Shepard, 34, to complete his undergraduate degree and to reach an important professional goal. Shepard had been an enlisted man in the Marines for thirteen years, but was unable to qualify for commissioned officer status until he had earned an undergraduate degree. With only one humanities course left to complete, Shepard found his military schedule in constant conflict with local college and university offerings.

The young Marine had progressed as far as his junior year while studying for a degree in health care management at George Mason University in Fairfax, Va. After a brief interim, he resumed his studies through an off-campus degree program offered by Southern Illinois University at the military base in Bethesda, Md. Instructors came to the base every weekend for sixteen months. Shepard attended classes and finished a course every six weeks. When all that remained for Shepard to complete his undergraduate degree was a single humanities course, he was working full-time and the course he needed wasn't offered during the evening at local colleges.

"It was at that time that I found ME/U," said Shepard. "ME/U had sent information about its program to Southern Illinois University. The university evaluated it and said it was a good program." The course, "Humanities through the Arts," was offered through ME/U by Colorado State University. It focused on how humans express themselves through the arts and included segments on art, music, cinema, architecture and literature. "I videotaped the program and watched it whenever I could," continued Shepard. "It was a great way to take the course."

Shepard claims his relationship with his Colorado-based instructor added to the learning experience. "Even though it was a long-distance relationship through correspondence and telephone calls, the student-teacher contact added a lot to the course. If you're not in class, you want to make sure you're not missing something. The instructor sent her biography and a photograph. We got to know each other during the class."

Shepard finally received his Bachelor of Science degree in health care management from Southern Illinois University in 1989 and was able to graduate with his class at Bethesda. "I was enlisted for thirteen years," said Shepard, "but it's because of the degree that I got my commissioned officer status, Ensign."

Twyla Hall, physically challenged student
Woodleaf, North Carolina

Twyla Hall, 30, has been equally tenacious in overcoming obstacles in her pursuit of an undergraduate degree.

Hall was born with a physical disability that severely restricts her ability to move about. Nevertheless, she was able to attend public school in Woodleaf, N.C., with the encouragement and logistical support of her parents. With the school's approval, her father constructed ramps and rails at the school to facilitate the use of a series of carts he had built so she could be pushed to her classes. By 1978, Hall had graduated with the rest of her high school class and was college bound.

The determined young woman had always planned to attend St. Andrews Presbyterian College in the nearby town of Laurinberg, the only college in the area with special facilities for the handicapped. Although she was accepted into the college, no dormitory space was available for her because so many other physically disabled students had applied. Hall decided to consider other colleges.

The University of North Carolina at Greensboro (UNCG) was her second choice; she enrolled, with a major in biology. Hall used an electric golf cart to get to and from classrooms, but the campus was large and she often had to be pushed home from classes. In addition, a multitude of stairs that daily confronted her took a long time to climb and frequently exhausted her.

"Steps were really a big hassle for me. I couldn't take a full academic load because I had to consider the time between classes. Once I had a science class on the fourth floor. After each day of that class, I was beat. At this regular college, I always felt as though I wasn't equal to the other students. I couldn't apply my best effort in class because I was always tired from climbing steps all day. Walking on crutches is a strenuous activity. The first week at UNCG I dropped 20 pounds. I had never seen so many steps."

The process of maneuvering between dorm and classroom finally became too much of a physical and logistics burden. As a first-semester junior, Hall withdrew from college, extremely upset by being unable to finish. "I left not knowing what else to do," she explained. "I hated that I couldn't finish my degree. It had been my lifetime dream to graduate from college." She tried attending classes at a local private college, but the school was not designed to handle the needs of handicapped students. Although she enjoyed her coursework, Hall eventually withdrew from this school, too.

Shortly thereafter, Hall was watching a satellite-delivered program on the family television when she happened across a classroom-like program. The man on screen, a professor, was discussing Einstein's theory of relativity. The course, being delivered by ME/U, was provided by Washington State University in Pullman. Hall contacted ME/U and enrolled in her first telecourse. She chose statistics, which she felt would aid her in her work as an insurance clerk in the family business.

Hall has now completed math and conversational Spanish classes in addition to her statistics coursework and plans to complete her degree. Hall noted that her professors "make you feel like you're part of a class. If you have a problem, they give you an 800 number to call. It's not a big deal to pop a tape in. It's meant a lot to me and to my parents. It's an unconventional way to go to college, but I feel very fortunate that I found ME/U. It was the only way I could do it."

A senior now, Hall and her parents plan to drive to Ohio State University for graduation so she can receive her diploma on campus. "We have a saying in our family: 'a winner never quits and a quitter never wins.' My mother always encourages me to finish whatever I start. She insists that I never give up because things look rough for me. That just isn't something we Halls do."

Kelly Matzenbacher, MBA student
Baton Rouge, Louisiana

Kelly Matzenbacher, a 29-year-old account manager with Xerox Corporation in Baton Rouge, La., had already completed his undergraduate degree and was trying to find a way to fit MBA coursework into his busy schedule, a way that didn't necessitate regular on-campus class attendance. Matzenbacher became one of the first students to enroll in the MBA degree program offered by Colorado State University on Mind Extension University.

Matzenbacher had previously enrolled in an MBA program at Louisiana State University in Baton Rouge, but was unable to complete his studies because, as he points out, "My schedule didn't coincide with theirs." The ME/U program appealed to him "because it was flexible. Xerox and other corporations value the MBA, and this is a rare opportunity for me to get it." Married and the father of two young children, Matzenbacher studies weekends and early in the morning.

A main consideration for Matzenbacher was the tendency of large corporations to move their employees to various locations throughout the country. By studying for an MBA via cable television, Matzenbacher explains, he won't have to worry about being transferred and, in the process, losing credit hours.

"I feel a bit like a guinea pig," he said. "Everyone, including my co-workers at Xerox, is interested in this new way to pursue MBA studies. It's a new concept."

Like Matzenbacher, other MBA students at ME/U and those considering enrolling cite flexibility and scheduling as factors that attract them to the program. Larry Forness, 45, a management, tax and financial consultant from Denver, Colo., is considering getting his MBA via cable for these two reasons. "I know I won't be able to go onsite or take courses at night. I wouldn't be able to commit to specific class times. Given my demanding schedule, I need a flexible day-by-day, week-by-week program so I can do coursework whenever I have free time. You can't do that in a campus setting."

Carolyn Sharp, lifelong learner
Norwood, Colorado

Carolyn Sharp has plenty of free time, but no nearby campus at which to attend classes. Although she loves living in small, rural Norwood, Colo., it's 150 miles away from the nearest city, Grand Junction. Life in Norwood can be isolating, says 71-year-old Sharp, who doesn't drive and lives too far out in the country to receive radio or broadcast television signals. Reflecting on the beauty and peacefulness of her surroundings, Sharp notes, "The only thing I lack here is intellectual stimulation."

Things changed, however, when Sharp's sister gave her a satellite dish. Her new television was able to receive a host of satellite-delivered programming, including ME/U. In 1988, she recalls, "I had already been boning up, doing some history research on my own, and I wanted to take a class. I took 'Humanities Through the Arts,' and it was a wonderful experience."

The course was especially interesting to Sharp, who had studied art in college and worked as a portrait painter until failing eyesight led her to writing. Mind Extension University's art course also helped Sharp with an ongoing project she's working on: a chronological (rather than alphabetical) arrangement of the encyclopedia as part of a new way to organize history. Explains Sharp, "The course pulled together everything I've learned in my 71 years. It corroborated what I believed, that the arts—theater, painting, sculpture—are the way we learn about history.''

Like many long-distance students, Sharp corresponded with her professor by mail and phone. They developed an excellent rapport, and her instructor even took an interest in her extracurricular work, reviewing parts of Sharp's encyclopedia. ''The teaching and class presentations were like nothing I'd ever seen,'' recalls Sharp. ''The visual effects were wonderful: you saw it, felt it, and heard it. It was so different from just reading a book.'' Sharp even became something of a celebrity, when Colorado State University sent a television crew to interview her about her work.

Although Sharp originally considered finishing her undergraduate degree through ME/U, she abandoned the idea because she felt it would take too long. She is currently auditing an ME/U French language class, however, as well as courses in history and physics, and she plans to continue pursuing her love of learning and understanding.

Mico Perales, MIT student
Nordheim, Texas

Mico Perales in now a sophomore electrical engineering student on full scholarship at the Massachusetts Institute of Technology (MIT) in Cambridge, Mass. However, not long ago he was a high school student in the tiny south Texas town of Nordheim, population 369, wondering if he would ever be able to achieve his dream of becoming an engineer.

Like many other small rural towns, Nordheim had difficulty finding teachers qualified to teach basic courses and willing to relocate to its geographically remote area. Finding teachers who could lead the advanced science and math classes required for Perales to compete for a spot at MIT seemed nearly impossible. However, his high school was able to support the young man's academic goals by using telecourses to provide an advanced curriculum of science, math, and foreign languages. In his junior and senior years, Perales took five TI-IN classes, ranking as the top student nationally in two of them.

Perales credits his advanced science and math telecourses— courses that many small rural schools find difficult to offer—

with providing the background he needed for acceptance to MIT. According to this bright engineering student, distance learning allowed him to develop intellectual skills commensurate with those of students from across the nation. Now he is pursuing his dream of a degree in electrical engineering and a profession in the field of robotics.

Jeremy Dilbeck, high school student
Murphy, North Carolina

Murphy, N.C., a small community in the extreme western corner of the state, has only 400 students in its kindergarten-through-high-school school system. And yet, as Hiwassee Dam High School sophomore Jeremy Dilbeck found, the school system made a commitment to not let its small size compromise the quality of education available to its students. Once limited by a narrow school curriculum, the high school decided to offer gifted students like Dilbeck advanced courses such as trigonometry, calculus, marine science, Latin, and Japanese via distance learning.

By taking part in many of TI-IN's academically advanced courses, Dilbeck was able to win a statewide competition for a summer scholarship to study social science at the Governor's School, a summer residential program for gifted students from throughout the state.

After completing the program, Dilbeck went on to the North Carolina School of Science and Math in Durham, a two-year accelerated high school for high academic achievers. Passing tough entrance exams and personal interviews, Dilbeck received a scholarship from the school and will live on campus for his junior and senior years.

This gifted young man plans to go on to college after completing his studies at the School of Science and Math. Although still undecided as to what area of expertise he will choose to pursue, Dilbeck is certain of one thing: distance education made possible many of the options he is currently considering.

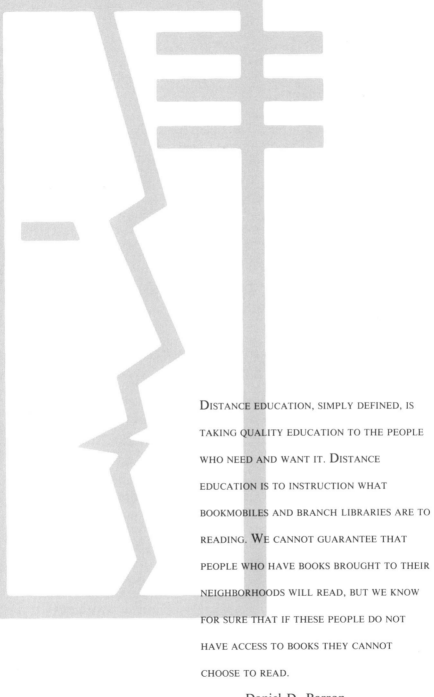

DISTANCE EDUCATION, SIMPLY DEFINED, IS
TAKING QUALITY EDUCATION TO THE PEOPLE
WHO NEED AND WANT IT. DISTANCE
EDUCATION IS TO INSTRUCTION WHAT
BOOKMOBILES AND BRANCH LIBRARIES ARE TO
READING. WE CANNOT GUARANTEE THAT
PEOPLE WHO HAVE BOOKS BROUGHT TO THEIR
NEIGHBORHOODS WILL READ, BUT WE KNOW
FOR SURE THAT IF THESE PEOPLE DO NOT
HAVE ACCESS TO BOOKS THEY CANNOT
CHOOSE TO READ.

—Daniel D. Barron,
School Library Journal,
November 1989

MIND EXTENSION UNIVERSITY
The Education Network™

TELECOURSES AND EDUCATORS

The role of ME/U in education is to augment, not sup-
plant, traditional education systems. Schools, colleges, and
universities offer on-site students a rich, communal learning
experience unsurpassed by any other educational configura-
tion. Mind Extension University's goal is to generate interest
and excitement about education generally and to encourage its
pursuit on both an individual and broad-scale basis.

In order to create an alternative means for delivering
education to students, we have created an electronic pipeline
for learning. This pipeline will enable America's schools to
extend their resources beyond the campus-bound classroom,
to offer educational opportunity where previously none existed.
Simultaneously, it allows students to reach out and receive
education resources from beyond their classrooms.

As part of its ongoing effort to support local educational
institutions, ME/U has established the Student Registrar Referral Program. This program informs potential students (who
have called ME/U for information about its courses) about
other educational programs offered by their local colleges and
universities. The Student Registrar Referral Program gener-
ates thousands of referrals of potential students to local colleges
and universities, thus supporting the region's educational institutions. Rather than competing with local schools, ME/U's role
is to complement them by delivering otherwise unavailable

course materials to them and by providing educational opportunity for students who would otherwise have none. The purpose of ME/U is to deliver education to students for whom access to traditional educational structures is either difficult or impossible.

EDUCATORS' CONCERNS

Distance education has been proving itself as a viable learning technology for years in America and in such geographically remote areas as South Australia and northwestern Canada. Nevertheless, many academicians resist accepting telecourses as a teaching tool. Often this resistance stems from past experiences with early televised educational experiments or lack of awareness about advances in telecourse instructional design and production.

In recent years numerous studies have compared the academic performance of telecourse students with that of in-class students. Although the results of these studies should not be considered definitive, the preliminary data comparing telecourse students with in-class students indicate that "no significant difference" exists between the performance of the two.[1]

Chicago's Citywide College has undertaken several studies to test the effectiveness of telecourses. Its research, experimentally controlled and conducted by distinguished educators from across the country, has demonstrated that home-based students tend to equal or surpass the performance of their on-campus counterparts of comparable age and ability.

These and other studies have shown that a motivated, committed student will learn as well through one delivery medium as through another, provided the course and delivery are well designed and executed. In fact, over the years telecourses have been placed under the academic curriculum committee's microscope far more often than any customary on-campus course. If telecourses had not passed critical academic review, they would not be around today, much less growing in use.

Human nature being what it is, teachers, like the rest of us, embrace change cautiously and with a healthy amount of skepticism. In this context, it might be helpful to remember that when computers were introduced in the workplace, many individuals feared they would be replaced by the new machines. On the contrary, today's office workers find that their skills, rather than being replaced by technology, have been extended by it. Computers are now relied on as tools that enable workers to reach higher levels of productivity and effectiveness. Telecourses can play the same role in the educational arena: extending the reach of our teachers, raising their productivity, increasing their effectiveness.

TELECOURSES AS A TEACHING TOOL

Many teachers have difficulty acknowledging that a telecourse in which the student views faculty-delivered instruction at a distance can be as effective as instruction in a traditional classroom setting where the instructor and students interact face-to-face.

As noted previously, distance education evaluations performed over the past ten years have consistently documented the effectiveness of telecourse learning experiences. Therefore, although the approach to instruction has traditionally been "point to point," in which the instructor speaks with students face-to-face, it is now necessary to supplement this approach with a "point to multipoint" system (which is classic cable-television system architecture). In this situation, the instructor may still be in the front of the classroom, but students can number in the millions and can be anywhere in the world.

Expanding the reach of our teachers will continue to be one of distance education's most important goals, for there are too many people today who cannot be present in the class-room where instruction is being delivered and too many students in schools where the necessary teachers do not exist. Therefore, teaching must become accessible from a distance; we can no longer be constrained by walls or by teachers' locations.

AUTHORSHIP

Another source of resistance to telecourse teaching is the "not developed here" or "not developed by me" response. Even though many telecourses rely on advisory boards that include peer reviewers and experts on the course's content, many people in the academic community are still reluctant to use someone else's materials. This is understandable; most instructors are initially most comfortable using their own material and presentation style.

Some instructors have overcome this hesitation to accept telecourses developed by others by adding their own video segments, called "wraparounds," to the existing package. Other instructors, realizing that they use textbooks developed by others and add their own supplemental material, feel that the criteria for using someone else's video material should be similar to that for using someone else's print material: if the academic quality is strong, the material can be useful. This makes the acceptance decision an issue of quality, rather than authorship.

QUALITY OF COURSE DESIGN

There is sometimes concern about the quality of instruction in today's telecourses among teachers who remember the early, "talking head" televised classes. Initial experiments with televised classes used a single, fixed camera aimed at the front of the classroom. Viewers lost sight of instructors who moved out of the camera's range and could see only the backs of the students in the classroom. It was often difficult for viewers to see clearly what was written on the chalkboard.

The basic problem with these early telecourse efforts was that the instructor focused on those in the classroom and ignored the needs of the distant student. Fortunately, advances in telecourse design have addressed these issues. Whereas early telecourse faculty typically had only themselves and occasional graduate students to rely on for design creativity and expertise, today's well-designed teleclasses incorporate the work of several skilled people, such as instructional designers, educational technologists, and television production specialists.

Today's telecourse instructors have learned to speak to distant students as though they were present in the classroom, and are better prepared to address their distance learners' needs through such aids as study guides to bridge the video and text material. Technological advances such as phone-mail systems and computer bulletin boards have been especially useful in facilitating student-teacher communication.

STUDENT-TEACHER INTERACTION

In distance education, students often receive information in a time-delayed manner rather than in "real time." Some teachers object to this delay because of the resulting loss of spontaneous feedback from the distance learner. While it is true that some immediate interaction may be sacrificed with telecourses, most distance learners cite the benefits of taped instruction as greatly outweighing the drawback of lack of spontaneity.

Videotaping teleclasses, the most common method of time-delayed delivery of instruction, has proved to be an effective way for distant students to review a concept for better understanding or to review selected material. It is especially helpful in alleviating students' concerns about whether they caught all the important points in their notes; the lesson will always be there for them on videotape.

Flexible scheduling is less of an issue for telecourses delivered to elementary and secondary schools. These courses, which can also be videotaped, offer instead the benefits of live, interactive presentation. Consequently, the full array of advanced communications technologies can be deployed to provide a dramatic and participatory educational experience.

"HANDS-ON" LEARNING SITUATIONS

Some academics have questioned the across-the-board applicability of telecourse learning. Certain course materials lend themselves to distance learning using today's technology better than others. For example, there is currently no technology that would enable distance students to take the laboratory component of courses for which they are required to have "hands-on" experience. Several solutions are under consideration to address this issue. For example, an alternative now being explored is the use of facilities at other institutions, which would involve setting up a network of lab sites where students could go to finish the required work and to gain the hands-on experience necessary to understand the material.

LIBRARY SUPPORT

Mastery of any subject includes the ability to navigate easily among the subject's reference works and major information resources, be they published, on-line through computer databases, or available in some other format. This skill, called "information literacy," is central to subject research and informed analysis (as well as increasingly important in day-to-day living).[2] Only when students understand how to use a subject's range of information resources are they able to move beyond the structured distillations of textbooks into the wealth of free-flowing ideas available in such resources as conference proceedings, master's and doctoral theses, association findings, industry analyses and journal reports. We agree strongly with educators that information literacy is central to the dialogue of learning. Alvin Toffler noted it in *Future Shock* twenty years ago in his statement, "Tomorrow's illiterate will not be the man who can't read; he will be the man who has not learned how to learn."[3]

On-campus students can explore these resources in their college or university libraries. For many distance education students, however, the most convenient research facility is a local public or community college library. Although these libraries may possess far fewer resources than standard academic libraries, they are usually able to provide guidance on the resources for a given subject and to obtain most of the materials needed through interlibrary loan.

Too many distance education students, however, face either an underfunded local library with few materials appropriate to their studies, or no library whatsoever. Physically challenged students may find library buildings as much like obstacle courses as local campuses.

Although we have achieved the goal of taking the teacher to the student, we are still working on the challenge of delivering the library's supporting resources into the home, school, and workplace. ME/U is currently working with the library community to help resolve this issue and is pursuing ways to make significant library resources available to the students ME/U serves.

MAKING THE TRANSITION

As more teachers use the techniques of telecourse education, they will devise their own solutions to the problems of distance education. Today's schools, in fact, are increasingly investing in the technologies that will deliver greater learning opportunities to their students. According to results published by the education research group Quality Education Data (QED) in their recent survey, *1990–1991 Educational Technology Trends,* 26 percent of the 1,262 U.S. school districts surveyed are currently using some form of distance education (an 18 percent increase from last year), and 57 percent of respondents planned to be using it by 1992. The QED survey results further indicated that distance learning is most frequently used in secondary education and that schools are receiving programming by means of both cable and satellite (81.6 percent receive cable television and 13.8 percent have satellite dishes). The subjects most in demand are foreign languages, social studies, and mathematics.[4]

An increasing number of elementary through secondary school educators understand that by integrating educational technologies into the teaching/learning equation, they benefit their students in another, critically important way. Distance education uses the communications technologies, the tools, of the information age. Students who are comfortable using these technologies will be better prepared to function in what Marshall McLuhan called "the Electronic Surround." These students will not be confused or intimidated by a workplace environment that includes computers, facsimile machines, audiographics, teleconferencing, and video-based training.

At the higher education level, various solutions are already being implemented: for example, fax machines are now transmitting assignments between instructors and students, while computer and phone lines are allowing "real time" interaction on student/faculty bulletin boards.

As distance educators incorporate new technology or innovative uses of current technology into their teaching, these benefits will continue to enlarge the student base for whom telecourse learning is a viable education alternative.

NEW TECHNOLOGICAL TOOLS

Technological advances will overcome many perceived obstacles. Today's communications and information technology industries are reconfiguring the way information moves through our society; what was impossible five years ago is mainstream today. These developments will affect the delivery of education in major ways still to unfold. Among these advances are:

- fiber optic delivery of two-way audio, data, and video;
- computer-based conferencing with "bulletin board" capabilities;
- interactive video capable of handling many laboratory requirements;
- compressed video, which will require less bandwidth than is currently used, facilitating greater use of video instruction;
- videotrax, a technology that allows data to be transmitted in a standard broadcast format via a video modem, enabling data to be sent before or after a telecourse cablecast; and
- high-definition television (HDTV) for use in laboratory work, allowing more precise presentation of small objects and activities to large numbers of students.

At the elementary and secondary levels, today's distance learning systems are often "hybrids, combining several technologies, such as satellite, Instructional Television Fixed

Services (ITFS), microwave, cable, fiber optic, and computer connections.'' Additionally, ''New developments in computer, telecommunications, and video technologies continue to expand the choices, and new strides in interconnecting systems are being made regularly.''[5]

Frequently, the distance learning system involves one-way video combined with two-way audio, the return link usually provided by the universally available and reliable telephone. The televised image of the teacher is seen in classrooms throughout the country, but the teacher does not see the students. Communication, which is ongoing while the class is ''in session,'' takes place by telephone. It enables students from Pensacola to Portland to benefit from each other's questions and answers, and it provides the teacher with an immediate sense of whether the instruction has been understood. The audio component may also include a ''homework hotline,'' which students can call for help with specific subjects or questions.

Other recent advances have made two-way graphics inter-activity possible through the use of two-way computer links. Audiographics, i.e., the use of computer-based technologies such as graphics tablets (a special digitized pad with a special pen), keypads (keyboards), scanners, printers, specially tailored fax machines, and similar types of equipment, allows even more classroom interactivity to take place, further enriching the learning experience. The computer screen in essence becomes an ''electronic blackboard.''

Add to these technologies the options available with video discs, optical discs, voice synthesizers, and CD-ROM, and it becomes apparent that the education environment is changing rapidly.

NEW COALITIONS

Across the nation, the public is becoming increasingly aware of the need for change in America's educational system. Since *A Nation at Risk* first documented the crisis in American education in 1987,[6] hundreds of reports have been issued, books published, and committees convened to address the declining state of American education. President George Bush, "the Education President," has called for a comprehensive, long-range plan to radically upgrade the quality of education available to all Americans, regardless of race, gender, or income. Educators, like the rest of us, understand that none of us can afford to resist technological tools that increase our professional productivity. The need for change is evident from Main Street to Wall Street, and no group is more aware of that need than our nation's educational leaders.

The drive to introduce distance learning alternatives in elementary through secondary education is spreading throughout the country. Although until recently few states had plans to explore distance education for elementary and secondary classes, today all fifty states have at least some commitment to distance education programs. The effects of this trend are wide-ranging and potentially of great benefit to both students and educators throughout the country. As noted in *Linking for Learning:*

> New coalitions across state and district boundaries, new networks of educators and geographically dispersed schools receiving programming from common providers exemplify changing relationships in the education community. Educators involved in interactive instruction, computer networking, and instructional television, although developing separately, are coming together. Connections now being established across geographic, instructional, and institutional boundaries provide opportunities for collaboration and resource sharing among many groups for the coming years.[7]

RECONFIGURING EDUCATIONAL DELIVERY

Much of the technological infrastructure for distance learning is in place, but it needs to be connected. Much of what is probable is made possible by satellite delivery systems, cable television systems, various consumer products such as VCRs, computers and their associated software packages and modems, broadcast media, and the limited but ubiquitous telephone.

What is required now in terms of the country's educational needs is cooperation. Cooperation among cable operators, satellite-delivered networks, telephone companies, broadcasters, libraries, educators, and others. To the extent possible we must all act in concert to ensure equality of access to high-quality educational opportunity in this country. Regardless of the evolving agenda of competing technologies, education must stand above these issues.

Although each of the technologies discussed above was initially relegated to a minor role in the traditional approach to teaching, teachers are now integrating them into the mainstream of the educational process. The technologies have been integrated to the greatest extent in elementary and secondary schools, where teachers have traditionally emphasized using the latest advances to improve teaching skills whenever possible. Additionally, teacher shortages at all levels from kindergarten through high school have forced certain school districts to hire technology instead of teachers. In this instance, the capabilities of educational technologies have by necessity become part of the teaching process.

Credit must be given to the far-sighted decision by such companies as Xerox, Apple, IBM, and software manufacturers to place, at little or no cost, their equipment, computers, and software in classrooms across America over the past several years. This generosity allowed both students and teachers to become familiar with the opportunities offered by computerized instruction and to incorporate this technology into the teaching process. The cable television industry, through its Alliance for Education, is currently orchestrating the wiring of the nation's schools, thereby adding yet another tool for delivering quality education throughout the country.

TELECOURSES AND THE CLASSROOM OF THE NINETIES

America cannot afford to employ teachers whose methods and skills do not keep pace with the demands and tools of today's educational environment. More and more of our country's educators are embracing this reality and are committed to using advanced educational technologies to enrich and extend the learning experience. These are the teachers who will lead our students into the twenty-first century.

Part of the challenge is to explore the link between effective uses of technology and effective instruction. Another part is to train teachers in the technology so they can comfortably incorporate it into their curriculum. This may include in-service training for practicing teachers, programs for new teachers, and ongoing research to document the effects of these teaching technologies. As noted by the editors of *Linking for Learning:*

> If distance education is to play an even greater role in improving the quality of education, it will require expanded technology; more linkages between schools, higher education, and the private sector; and more teachers who use technology well.[8]

A recent survey of more than 800 teachers of fifth- through eighth-graders indicated that a majority of teachers recognize the benefits of video-based learning. The survey, carried out by Yankelovich Clancy Shulman, found that 96 percent of the teachers had access to television sets in their schools, 95 percent to VCRs, and 43 percent to cable television. Videotapes and/or television programs were considered appropriate classroom teaching aids by 94 percent of the respondents. Nearly two thirds of the teachers reported using television and VCRs at least once a week, with 50 percent using cable as often.[9]

In a survey commissioned by the National Education Association (NEA), the nation's largest teachers' union, responses indicated that 57.6 percent of U.S. elementary and secondary schools (approximately 2.5 million teachers) use some form of educational video programming, whether from network, public broadcasting, or cable television.[10]

America's teachers have seen the future and understand the role of televised education in it. As NEA President Keith Geiger observed, "There has been a virtual tidal wave of teachers' turning to video and television technology to help students learn." Once used strictly for entertainment, television is now being used to free educators and students from what Geiger describes as "the pedagogical prison of the two covers of the textbook, the four walls of the classroom and the six hours of the school day."[11]

Technical training for educators cannot be the sole responsibility of colleges, universities, and school districts. All of us are embedded in this evolution, and all must contribute. Partnerships between those who develop the technology and those who use it are needed. This will require linking different technologies in a variety of ways to fit the needs of different groups of educators. The variables to consider are numerous, and the groups of people working out the concepts and details will be varied.

Americans have no choice but to undertake this task, and we must move quickly to ensure that as many people as possible have access to quality education. That education must be timely, and it must be accessible to students without undue disruption to their lives. This may require that many, many barriers come down, but so be it. The words of Richard Saul Wurman in *Information Anxiety* are stingingly true: "The issue is learning, not schools."[12]

Since Harvard first opened its doors in 1636, there has been little change in our higher education structure, a system borrowed from our English ancestors centuries ago. We know, however, that tomorrow will not be like yesterday. The information society brings new problems, and new methods and new tools must be used to resolve them.

The electronic pipeline will be an increasingly important piece of tomorrow's educational technology. Our task is to learn not only how to use this technology but how to use it wisely and effectively. Working together, we can use it to educate and to empower. This is the goal of Mind Extension University: The Education Network.

---

[1]Numerous studies have evaluated the effectiveness of telecourses as an educational technology. For results of several of those studies, see the following articles: D. L. Morehouse, M. L. Hoaglund, and R. H. Schmidt, "Interactive television: Findings, issues and recommendations," paper presented at the Vision for Rural and Small Schools Conference sponsored by the Illinois Board of Education, September 17, 1987, Springfield, Ill.; N. Whittington, "Is instructional television educationally effective? A research review," *The American Journal of Distance Education,* Vol. 1, No. 1, pp. 47-57; D. Wydra, "The Pennsylvania audiographic teleteaching project," address delivered at the Eighth Annual Conference for Administrators of Community Schools, December 1, 1987, Lubbock, Tex.; and Michael Moore, "Effects of distance learning: A summary of the literature," Office of Technology Assessment contractor report, May 1989.

2For a thorough discussion of information literacy, see Patricia Senn Breivik and E. Gordon Gee, *Information Literacy: Revolution in the Library* (New York: MacMillan Publishing Company for American Council on Education, 1989).

3Alvin Toffler, *Future Shock* (New York: Bantam Books, 1970), p. 414.

4Quality Educational Data (QED), *1990-1991 Educational Technology Trends.* Available from: QED, 1600 Broadway, Denver, CO 80202.

5United States Congress, Office of Technology Assessment, *Linking for Learning: A New Course for Education,* OTA-SET-430 (Washington, DC: U.S. Government Printing Office, November 1989), p. 8.

6*A Nation at Risk: The Full Account,* The National Commission on Excellence in Education (Cambridge, Mass.: USA Research, 1984).

7*Linking for Learning,* p. 26.

8*Linking for Learning,* p. 4.

9"Teaching tool," *Cable Television Business,* October 15, 1990, p. 10.

10"PTV is easily most widely viewed TV network in U.S. schools," *Public Broadcasting Report,* July 20, 1990.

11"Teaching tool," p. 10.

12Richard Saul Wurman, *Information Anxiety* (New York: Doubleday, 1989), p. 123.

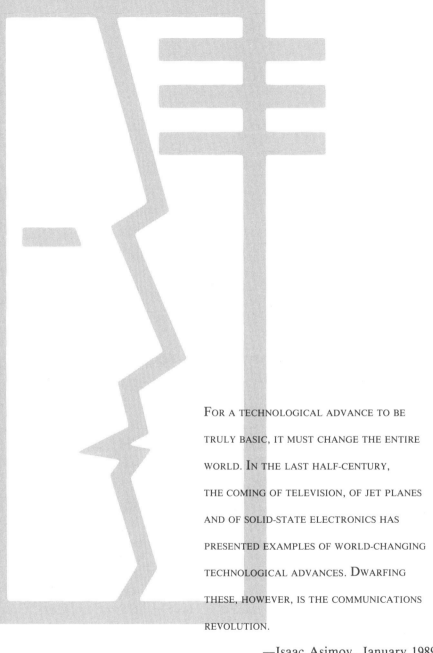

FOR A TECHNOLOGICAL ADVANCE TO BE
TRULY BASIC, IT MUST CHANGE THE ENTIRE
WORLD. IN THE LAST HALF-CENTURY,
THE COMING OF TELEVISION, OF JET PLANES
AND OF SOLID-STATE ELECTRONICS HAS
PRESENTED EXAMPLES OF WORLD-CHANGING
TECHNOLOGICAL ADVANCES. DWARFING
THESE, HOWEVER, IS THE COMMUNICATIONS
REVOLUTION.

—Isaac Asimov, January 1989

EPILOGUE

Book shelves strain under the weight of books sounding the alarms of the information revolution and the speed at which new information is being generated. The important fact to realize, however, is that at the end of the day this information must be dealt with by an electrochemical contraption that weighs 3 pounds, more or less, takes up about half a cubic foot of space, runs on glucose at about 25 watts, processes information at the rate of approximately 100 quadrillion operations per second, looks like a big walnut, and is the world's first wet computer: the human brain. That brain is under siege. It is being bombarded from all sides by torrents of new information.

Mind Extension University is a pro-active, entrepreneurial effort to empower the individual through education, and in that manner to contribute to the conversion of information into knowledge, understanding and wisdom. It was designed as a partial solution to a growing problem: how to provide educational opportunities to the increasing number of people who want education but for a multitude of reasons are unable to attend on-campus classes. It was also designed to deliver classroom instruction from highly qualified teachers, remotely located, to classrooms in schools across America. ME/U was created as a way to deliver education to people instead of people to education.

Mind Extension University was also designed to enlighten through education any viewer, registered student or not, who has an interest in learning. To create, on cable television, an educational community. It is intended to create interest and excitement about education generally and to encourage lifelong learning.

Mind Extension University is part of the entrepreneurial evolution of cable television. It focuses not on what cable was or is but rather on what it can become. It is based on the concept of actively engaging the minds of its viewers in a positive way. Technological advances have created a communications environment where vast amounts of information can be delivered inexpensively. An environment where time and distance are erased. Both individuals and committees, in great numbers, have defined many of our educational problems. Continuing study and dialogue may be necessary, but it is clearly time for those who can act to act. To act boldly, now.

If there are 50 students in an average classroom, then cable television's 55 million subscribers, multiplied by 2.5 people per home, represent a potential school with 2,750,000 classrooms. Cable television can be of enormous help in today's environment. It is simply a matter of acting.

The television industry must respond to the country's needs. We must commit. Although cable television is improving the situation, we as a nation cannot afford the television environment described recently by media critic Duane Elgin:

> Less than 5% of prime-time TV is typically devoted to informational programming. We are entertainment rich and knowledge poor: at the very time our democracies face problems of marathon proportions, we're preparing for that marathon with a diet of junk food.[1]

Problems strain for resolution, and the means for resolution are now available to us. There is a strong sense of need in the air, and the environment is ripe for change. Many educators are eager to use the electronic tools of the information age, and their numbers expand daily. We must work together. There is a place for everyone in this undertaking.

Imagine the vibrant energy and intellect of Athens during the time of Socrates and Plato. The ghost of Athens is visible today.

It has been said that Plato, in all his strivings to imagine an ideal training school, failed to notice that Athens itself was a greater school than even he could dream of.

Let us notice *our* environment. It is time now to fuse our electronic tools of the information age with our great teaching institutions and repositories of information. It is time to create a nation that is, like Athens was, a great school. A place vibrant with interest and excitement about education. A place where educational opportunity is visible to all and hope is alive. A place that sees the wilderness of information as our new frontier.

MAKE ALL AMERICA A SCHOOL.
WORKING TOGETHER, WE CAN DO IT, NOW.

---

[1]Duane Elgin, "Sustainable television," *In Context,* No. 23, January 1990, p. 27.

SELECTED BIBLIOGRAPHY

Adler, Mortimer J. *Reforming Education; The Opening of the American Mind.* New York: Macmillan Publishing Company, 1977.

Bok, Derek. *Higher Learning.* Cambridge, Mass.: Harvard University Press, 1986.

Bolles, Richard N. *The Three Boxes of Life, and How to Get Out of Them.* Berkeley, Calif.: Ten Speed Press, 1978.

Botkin, James et al. *Global Stakes; The Future of High Technology in America.* Cambridge, Mass.: Ballinger Publishing Company, 1982.

Bowsher, Jack E. *Educating America; Lessons Learned in the Nation's Corporations.* New York: John Wiley & Sons, Inc., 1989.

Boyer, Ernest L. and Hechinger, Fred M. *Higher Learning in the Nation's Service.* Washington, D.C.: The Carnegie Foundation for the Advancement of Teaching, 1981.

Breivik, Patricia Senn and Gee, E. Gordon. *Information Literacy; Revolution in the Library.* New York: Macmillan Publishing Company for the American Council on Education, 1989.

Cetron, Marvin and O'Toole, Thomas. *Encounters with the Future: A Forecast of Life into the 21st Century.* New York: McGraw-Hill, 1982.

Dizard, Wilson P. Jr. *The Coming Information Age: An Overview of Technology, Economics, and Politics, Third Edition.* White Plains, NY: Longman Inc., 1989.

Durant, Will and Ariel. *The Lessons of History.* New York: Simon & Schuster, Inc., 1968.

Dychtwald, Ken and Flower, Joe. *Age Wave; The Challenges and Opportunities of an Aging America.* Los Angeles: Jeremy P. Tarcher, Inc., 1989.

Johnston, William B. and Packer, Arnold H. *Workforce 2000: Work and Workers for the Twenty-first Century.* Indianapolis, Ind.: Hudson Institute, Inc., 1987.

Kanter, Rosabeth Moss. *The Change Masters; Innovation and Entrepreneurship in the American Corporation.* New York: Simon & Schuster, Inc., 1983.

Kearns, David T. and Doyle, Denis P. *Winning the Brain Race; A Bold Plan to Make our Schools Competitive.* San Francisco, Calif.: Institute for Contemporary Studies, 1988.

Kelly, Kevin. Signal: *Communication Tools for the Information Age.* New York: Harmony Books, 1988.

Levine, Arthur and Associates. *Shaping Higher Education's Future.* San Francisco, Calif.: Jossey-Bass Publishers, 1989.

Linking for Learning: A New Course for Education. United States Congress, Office of Technology Assessment. Washington, D.C.: U.S. Government Printing Office, 1989.

Martel, Leon. *Mastering Change; The Key to Business Success.* New York: New American Library, 1986.

Merriam, Sharan B. and Cunningham, Phyllis M. *Handbook of Adult and Continuing Education.* San Francisco, Calif.: Jossey-Bass Publishers, 1989.

Naisbitt, John. *Megatrends: Ten New Directions Transforming our Lives.* New York: Warner Books, 1982.

A Nation at Risk: The Full Account. The National Commission on Excellence in Education. Cambridge, Mass.: USA Research, 1984.

Peters, Tom. *Thriving on Chaos; Handbook for a Management Revolution.* New York: Harper & Row, 1987.

Silber, John. *Straight Shooting; What's Wrong with America and How to Fix It.* New York: Harper & Row, 1989.

Sykes, Charles J. *ProfScam; Professors and the Demise of Higher Education.* Washington, D.C.: Regnery Gateway, 1989.

Toffler, Alvin. *Future Shock.* New York: Bantam Books, 1970.

Wurman, Richard Saul. *Information Anxiety.* New York: Doubleday, 1989.

To order additional copies of MAKE ALL AMERICA A SCHOOL, SECOND EDITION, complete the form below and send it, along with a check or money order for the appropriate amount, to:

Jones 21st Century, Inc.
9697 E. Mineral Ave.
Englewood, CO 80112

For discount information on purchases of ten or more books, please call (303) 792-3111.

MAKE ALL AMERICA A SCHOOL, SECOND EDITION

Jones 21st Century, Inc.
9697 E. Mineral Ave.
Englewood, CO 80112

Please send MAKE ALL AMERICA A SCHOOL, SECOND EDITION, to:

Name _____

Address _____

City _____

State _____ Zip _____

Number of copies _____ @ $9.95* each = _____

Postage and handling @ $2.50 each = _____

Total enclosed_____

*Introductory price

Thank you for your order!

STANDING ON THE SIDELINES

By the same author:

Four O'Clock Friday

STANDING ON THE SIDELINES

Original poems by John Foster

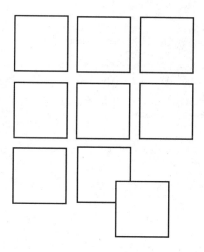

Oxford University Press

Oxford New York Toronto

Oxford University Press, Walton Street, Oxford OX2 6DP
Oxford New York Toronto
Delhi Bombay Calcutta Madras Karachi
Kuala Lumpur Singapore Hong Kong Tokyo
Nairobi Dar es Salaam Cape Town
Melbourne Auckland Madrid

and associated companies in
Berlin Ibadan

Oxford is a trade mark of Oxford University Press

Copyright © John Foster 1995
First published 1995

Illustrated by Debbie Cook

ISBN O 19 276135 8 (hardback)
ISBN O 19 276136 6 (paperback)

A CIP catalogue record for this book is available from the
British Library

Printed in Hong Kong

Contents

Tall story

Today, our teacher
Asked us to write
Lacrosse sticks in our English
Lesson. At least, that's what we thought

She said.
That's why most
Of us looked blank and
Replied, 'If it's all right with
You, we'd rather write high queues instead.'

Life's a spelling test

Life's a spelling test
When I ask you, 'What's your name?'
For I may spell it differently,
Although it sounds the same.

Are you Catherine with a C,
Or Katherine with a K,
Or Kathryn with a y,
Or Catharine with an a?

Is it Stephen with ph
Or Steven with a v?
Are you Glenn with double n?
Do I spell Ann(e) with an e?

Are you Sophie with ie
Or Sophy with a y?
Are you Jon without an h
Or Clare without an i?

Life's a spelling test,
It's your parents who're to blame.
What's on your birth certificate
Is how they spelt your name.

Doctors

Dr Aft is rough and ready.
Dr Unk's a bit unsteady.

Dr Omedary's got the hump.
Dr Ift's a snowy bump.

Dr Aught's a shivery chap.
Dr Owsy likes to nap.

Dr Um beats out a roll.
Dr Iver's in control.

Dr Agon's a fiery fighter.
Dr Acula's a late-night biter!

The day I became a vegetarian

When I was seven and a half,
I decided to become a vegetarian.

When I arrived home from school,
I told my mum.
'That's fine,' she said.
'It's up to you what you eat.
We're having meat.
The vegetables are over there.'

An hour later,
When Dad came home,
I sat down to eat
Like the rest of the family.
I'd decided to give up
Being a vegetarian.

Sarah, my sister, has asthma

Sarah, my sister, has asthma.
Sometimes, I wake up in the night
And hear her wheezing
In the bunk below.

I remember the time
I woke to hear her gasping for breath
And Mum had to call an ambulance.
They took her to the hospital
And kept her in for tests.

'She's allergic,' the doctor said.
'I expect she'll grow out of it.
Most young children do.'

Now she carries an inhaler
Everywhere she goes.

She gets annoyed when people
Try to stop her doing things.
She's always telling Grandma
To stop fussing.

'I'm not different,' she says.
'It's only asthma.
Lots of people have it.'

On Sports Day
Sarah came first in the high jump.
'You see, I'm not different,' she said.

Sarah, my sister, has asthma.
Sometimes I wake up in the night
And hear her wheezing
In the bunk below.

Wait for me

My brother Tim
Is three years older than me.

When I was six,
I could never keep up with him.
I remember
Running down the path after him
Shouting, 'Wait for me!
Wait for me!'

Since the accident,
Tim can't run any more.
Now, he sits in his chair,
Waiting for me
As I hurry on ahead
To open the gate
And help him down the steps.

Sisterly feelings

When my sister Gemma
was very, very ill,
I felt bad
because of all the attention
and all the presents she had.
Then, Gemma died
and all I felt
was very, very sad.

Just because you're my sister

Just because you're my sister,
Why should I do what you do?
Just because you're my sister,
Why should I behave like you?

Everyone goes on and on
About how well you've done,
About the exams you've passed
And all the trophies you've won.

Why can't they leave me alone?
Why can't everyone see
I don't want to be a copy of you,
I just want to be valued as me.

Talking to the wall

My sister sits in her own world
With her Walkman blaring away
And when we try to talk to her
She doesn't hear a word we say.

But when she wants to talk to us
She pulls her earphones out
And if we do not answer her
She stamps her foot and shouts.

'What makes you angry, Mum?'

'What makes you angry, Mum?' I asked.

'When people lie and cheat and steal.
But most of all people
who couldn't care less
how other people feel.'

Everything's fine

First, we missed the turning off the motorway.
Don't ask me how!
I'd fallen asleep in the back.
I was woken by the shouting
As they tried to blame each other.
We had to drive another twelve miles
To the next junction
And another twelve miles back.
By that time it was dark.
It took us another half-hour
To find the campsite.
It's down this narrow lane.
Half-way along we met another car.
The driver just sat there,
So we had to reverse
All the way back to the main road.
By the time we got to reception,
It was closed.
It took us twenty minutes
To find the warden.
He kept complaining
That he was off duty.
Then, he couldn't find our booking-form.
'We're full up,' he said,
'Apart from the overflow field
And we're not really supposed to use that
At this time of year.'

You can tell why it's called
The overflow field.
The mud's inches thick
And it's right next to the toilet block.
I've left them putting the tent up.
I'm just phoning to let you know
We've arrived safely
And everything's fine.

It's a dog's life

Mum says
Our dog's
Having an identity crisis.

Yesterday,
He went out into the garden,
Then tried to come back in
Through the cat-flap.

He jammed his head so tight,
No matter how hard
We pushed and pulled
It wouldn't budge.

In the end,
We had to call the fire brigade.

When Dad came home
He nearly had a fit,
When he saw
What they'd done to the door.

He called the dog
All sorts of names.
But when the dog jumped up
To beg for his evening walk,
Dad still took him.

It's not fair.
If I'd smashed the door,
I wouldn't have been allowed out
For at least two weeks!

Mrs Nugent's budgie

Yesterday,
Our neighbour Mrs Nugent
Accidentally sat on her budgie.
'How did it happen?' I asked.
'Was it flattened?' said Sally.
'Like on Tom and Jerry.'
'She'd let it out
For a fly around,' said Mum.
'And she sat down on the bed
Without noticing it was there.'
'Poor thing,' said Dad.
'It didn't stand much of a chance
With her on top of it.'
'It's not dead!' said Mum.
'It lay there stunned for a while,
Then started to twitch.
So she picked it up
And popped it back in its cage.
It looked fine when I saw it,
Except that its head
Is a bit on one side.'
'Will it be all right?' I asked.
'I expect so,' said Dad.
'It sounds a tough old bird,
Like Mrs Nugent!'

The price

There's a price for the eggs you eat,
It's the hens that have to pay,
Locked in their battery cages
Day after day after day.

'It's warm and dry,' the farmer says,
'There's plenty to drink and eat.'
But the sloping wire-mesh floor
Gives them deformed feet.

There's nowhere for them to perch.
It's hard to turn around.
They cannot spread their wings
Or forage for food on the ground.

'The profit margin's higher,'
I heard the farmer say.
'It's in everybody's interest
To keep the hens this way.'

There's a price for the eggs you eat,
It's the hens that have to pay,
Locked in their battery cages
Day after day after day.

Guided tour

'We do everything we can
To ensure that the animals
Do not suffer unnecessarily,'
Said the guide.
'Our methods of experimentation
Are constantly under review.
Take these rats, for example,
Until recently,
In order to test
The regenerative capacity
Of damaged nerve tissues,
It was necessary
To sever the nerves
Leading to one of their hind legs.
Now, a refinement of our technique
Enables us to carry out the experiment
By cutting only the nerve
To a single toe.'

'May I ask a question?'
Said a woman in a green raincoat.
'Am I to understand,
From what you just said,
That you are so concerned
About the welfare of these animals
That you no longer find it necessary
To cripple them?'

The perfect animal

Scientists in California claim to have created the perfect laboratory
animal – a mouse that can be implanted with human organs.
The Independent Magazine 20 April 1991.

'We have created,'
said the scientist,
'the perfect animal.'
He pointed proudly.
Behind the glass partition
stretched row upon row
of Perspex containers
full of mice,
stacked on the shelves like shoeboxes.
'Each of those mice
has been born without an immune system,
which means . . .'
(He paused for effect.)
'They are perfect for our purposes.
We are able to implant into them
the still-living tissue
of aborted foetuses,
and . . . ' (Again, the pause for effect.)
'They do not reject it!
All kinds of experiments
that were not possible before
are now possible.'

'Are there any drawbacks?'
asked a bespectacled young man.

'It's necessary,'
replied the scientist,
'to provide a germ-free environment,
to filter the air they breathe
and to feed them irradiated food.'

'Do you mean to say,'
said a woman in a green raincoat,
'that the only drawback
with your perfect animal
is that it cannot lead
a normal life?'

Pistol practice

The barrel glinted in the sunlight.
I watched
As my friend pinned up
The printed target –
A small black rabbit
With a ring of white circles
Marking the spot to shoot at –
'The best place for killing it.'

The barrel glinted in the sunlight.
I watched
As my friend took aim.
The printed target
Shivered with the impact.
'Got him!' my friend said,
Pointing to the clean white hole
In the centre of the circles.

The barrel glinted in the sunlight.
I watched
As my friend casually reloaded.
The printed target blurred.

Instead I saw
A rabbit caught in mid-leap
Stagger at the bullet's punch,
Then crash to the ground,
Limp and lifeless.

'Want a go?' my friend asked.

I turned and walked indoors.

Facts about air

Scientists say
That air consists
Of about 78% nitrogen and 21% oxygen,
Plus some carbon dioxide
And small amounts
Of the rare gases – helium, argon, and neon.

These are facts, I know.
But I also know
That when I go outside
On a spring morning
The air tastes as crisp
As a fresh lettuce
And that when I sit
On the patio
On a summer evening
The cool night air
Brushes my cheeks like a feather.

Summer storm

Light travels, said Miss,
Faster than sound.
Next time there's a storm,
When you see the lightning,
Start counting slowly in seconds.
If you divide
The number of seconds by three,
It will tell you
How many kilometres you are
From the centre of the storm.

Two nights later,
I was woken
By the lashing rain,
The lightning,
And the thunder's crash.

I lay,
Huddled beneath the sheet,
As the rain poured down
And lightning lit up the bedroom,
Slowly counting the seconds,
Listening for the thunder
And calculating the distance
As the storm closed in –

Until,
With a blinding flash
And a simultaneous ear-splitting crash,
The storm passed
Directly overhead,

And I shook with fright
As the storm passed on,
Leaving the branches shuddering,
And the leaves weeping.

What is water?

A magician
Transforming deserts
With a lick of its tongue.

A conjuror
Coating ponds with ice
Or brushing your cheek with mist.

A wild animal
Plunging over cliffs,
Breaking bridges and flooding valleys.

A healer
Quenching thirst,
Rekindling the seed's flame.

A slippery customer
Slithering through your fingers,
Always on the run.

Spells

I crackle and spit. I lick and leap higher.
This is the spell of the raging fire.

I clasp and I grasp. I grip in a vice.
This is the spell of torturing ice.

I claw and I scratch. I screech and I wail.
This is the spell of the howling gale.

I clash and I crash. I rip asunder.
This is the spell of booming thunder.

I whisper. I stroke. I tickle the trees.
This is the spell of the evening breeze.

I slither. I slide. I drift and I dream.
This is the spell of the murmuring stream.

What is a shooting star?

It is a sliver of silver
that has dropped out of a hole
in the pocket of the sky.

It is a priceless coin
that slipped through a giant's fingers
while he was counting his change.

It is a magic message
flashing briefly across the night's screen
before vanishing forever.

Moons

The new moon
Is curved like a banana –
A bright C
Stamped on the sky's black page.

The old moon
Is round like a grapefruit –
A shiny button
Sewn on the sky's dark coat.

November

November is a grey road
Cloaked in mist.
A twist of wood-smoke
In the gathering gloom.
A scurrying squirrel
Hoarding acorns,
A steel-grey river
Glinting in the twilight.
A grey rope
Knotted around a threadbare tree.

Winter

Whirling snow and whistling wind
Icy patterns on window panes
Numb fingers and freezing toes
Trees stripped bare
Earth bone-hard
Roaring fires and long, dark nights.

It's spring

It's spring
And the garden is changing its clothes,
Putting away
Its dark winter suits,
Its dull scarves
And drab brown overcoats.

Now it wraps itself in green shoots,
Slips on blouses
Sleeved with pink and white blossom,
Pulls on skirts of daffodil and primrose,
Snowdrop socks and purple crocus shoes,
Then dances in the sunlight.

In the still dark

In the still dark,
High above the meadow,
The barn owl hovers,
Ear flaps erect,
Listening.

In the still dark,
Down in the meadow,
The small brown fieldmouse
Crunches the corn husk,
Unsuspecting.

In the still dark,
High above the meadow,
The barn owl swivels,
With deadly precision
Pinpointing its prey.

In the still dark,
Down towards the meadow,
The barn owl
Plunges silently,
Talons outstretched.

In the still dark,
Down in the meadow,
The barn owl
Strikes.

Arctic skua

The Arctic skua
Is a bully bird.
Like a pirate
It patrols the seashore
On the lookout
For plunder.
Spotting a tern
With a fish in its beak,
It gives chase,
Mounting a relentless pursuit,
Until the tern,
Frightened and flustered,
Drops its catch.

The skua pounces.

Having tasted success,
The robber
Returns to its vigil,
Scanning the shoreline
For its next victim.

Christmas 1992

Under a threadbare blanket, on a mattress of stone,
A teenager shivers, cold and alone.

High on a mountainside, on a carpet of snow,
A refugee waits with nowhere to go.

Under a blistering sky, on a cushion of sand,
A starving child squats and holds out her hand.

TV Wars (1991 version)

We sat in our living-rooms and watched
With a mixture of awe and pride
As the bombs poured from the sky
And Iraqi soldiers died.

We sat in our living-rooms and watched
The scenes on the mountainside,
With a mixture of horror and guilt
As Kurdish families died.

We sat in our living-rooms and watched,
Feeling powerless we sighed,
As the Serbian troops advanced
And Croatian people died.

We sat in our living-rooms and watched,
'What else can we do?' we cried,
As we silently wrote out cheques,
Passing by on the other side.

'It isn't right to fight'

You said, 'It isn't right to fight,'
But when we watched the news tonight,
You shook your fist and said
You wished the tyrant and his cronies dead.
When I asked why,
If it's not right to fight,
You gave a sigh.
You shook your head
And sadly said,
'Sometimes a cause is just
And, if there is no other way,
Perhaps, you must.'

Who's to say?

(On the fiftieth anniversary of the battle of
El Alamein, October 1992)

Great-grandmother said:
'Fifty years ago today,
your great-grandfather was killed.
They say it was the battle
that turned the tide of the war –
the first great Allied victory.
Ten thousand of our young men died.
They calculated the sacrifice was worth it.
Who's to say?
All I know is,
if there had been no war,
he might still be here
today.'

One of the many

No more waiting for the knock on the door.
No more crouching on the cellar floor.

No more listening to the TV lies.
No more disguising the look in your eyes.

No more watching what you say on the phone.
No more the feeling that you're never alone.

No more editing every word that you say.
No more curfew at the end of each day.

No more censoring what you're able to know.
No more following wherever you go.

No more being told what to think, what to do,
Except to stand here, to wait in the queue –

One of the many, not one of the few,
A free refugee.

Olympic circles

While they circled the track,
Muscles straining, lungs bursting,
In search of gold,
Elsewhere, lips cracked, stomachs knotted,
Others trudged under the same sun
In search of food,
While overhead the vultures circled.

I dream of a time

I dream of a time

When the only blades are blades of corn
When the only barrels are barrels of wine
When the only tanks are full of water
When the only chains are chains of hands

I hope for a time . . .

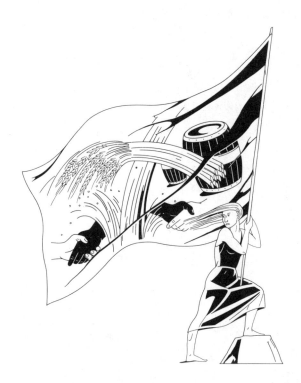

Sing a song of censorship

Sing a song of censorship, a pocketful of lies,
Four-and-twenty officers, each with eagle eyes,
Checking every column, forging every link –
Say thank you to the gentlemen who tell us what to
    think.

Beware the Smile-a-Lot

Beware the Smile-a-Lot
His welcome is not what it seems;
Behind his outstretched hand
He is cunningly hatching schemes.

Taking sides

We're canvassing opinions.
We'd simply like to know
Exactly where you stand,
How far you're prepared to go.

If it comes to the crunch,
What will you do?
Are you one of us?
Can we count on you?

We'd much appreciate it,
If you would just sign.
We knew you'd understand.
Here, on the dotted line.

Standing on the sidelines

I'm standing on the sidelines,
Practising with a ball,
Developing my skills,
Waiting for your call.

I'm standing on the platform,
Waving at each train,
Wondering if, and when or where
I'll catch a ride again.

I'm standing in the courtroom,
Accused of the crime
Of trying to scrape a living
While idly killing time.

I'm standing in the corridor.
I'm waiting in the queue.
I'd rather not be here,
But it's what I have to do.

Scene switching

Standing outside the Head's office,
I wish that I could fast forward
Through the scene
In which she's going to tell me off
And decide what punishment to give me.

Or that I could rewind the tape
To before break,
Then replay the scene
In which Tracey and I quarrelled.

Only this time, I'd play it differently.

The sporting spirit

On Sports Day, my friend Sally sat
With her back to the track,
Refusing to watch
Or fill in her programme.
'Who cares who wins?' she said,
And she read a magazine
Until Miss Evans snatched it from her,
Told her she was letting the side down
And sent her indoors
To write an essay on 'The sporting spirit.'

As I watched Sally stride off,
Head held high, towards our classroom,
I opened my programme
And wrote Sally's name in block capitals
Alongside the other winners.

Not the answer

Why is it
that when there's a fight
in the playground,
everyone gathers round
and starts taking sides,
even though most of them
don't know who started it
or what it's about?

Why is it
that when there's a fight
in the playground,
I join the others
and race to watch and cheer,
even though I know
deep down inside
fighting's not the answer?

And how was school today?

Each day they ask: And how was school today?
Behind my mask, I shrug and say OK.

Upstairs, alone, I blink away the tears
Hearing again their scornful jeers and sneers.

Hearing again them call me by those names
As they refused to let me join their games.

Feeling again them mock me with their glares
As they pushed past me rushing down the stairs.

What have I done? Why won't they let me in?
Why do they snigger? What's behind that grin?

Each day they ask: And how was school today?
Behind my mask, I shrug and say OK.

I dreamed a dolphin

Yesterday,
On the way to school,
I dreamed a dolphin
That cavorted happily all day,
Swimming and singing.

When I went through the school gates,
The nets ensnared me.
I spent the day
Wallowing in the shallows,
An ordinary fish.

Jane

I called for Jane as usual
But no one answered the door.
At registration Miss said:
'Jane's not in this class any more.'

Mum said she'd heard they'd moved away.
She did not know why or where.
I wonder what school Jane will go to now
And if she'll be happier there.

Dad

One Monday,
While we were at school,
He just packed a suitcase
And left.

Mum cried a lot.

Gran came to stay for a while.
She went on and on
About how much better it would be
Now that he'd gone.

We haven't heard from him since.

Sometimes,
I wonder where he is
And what he's doing.

I wonder if he
Ever thinks of me.

Every other Sunday

Every other Sunday,
I stand and wait
For Dad to pick me up
Down by the front gate.

If the weather's fine,
We visit the park or zoo.
When it rains, we sit in a café
Wondering what to do.

He asks me about school
And what I've done this week.
But everything's different now
And we find it hard to speak.

Every other Sunday,
Dead on half-past four
Dad drops me outside the house,
And waits till I've gone in the door.

Great-Grandad

Great-Grandad forgets
The time of the day,
Where he was going,
What he wanted to say.

Great-Grandad forgets
The day of the week.
He cannot recall
What we say when we speak.

Great-Grandad forgets
What he wants to do.
Sometimes when he sees me
He thinks that I'm you.

But Great-Grandad remembers
The relief and delight
The day the war ended
And they partied all night.

Great-Grandad remembers
How as a young man
He first met the girl
Who is now our great-gran.

Great-Grandad remembers
How things used to be
And I smile as he tells
His memories to me.

Great-Aunt Charlotte

Why don't you smile like you used to?
Why don't you think what you say?
Why do you dress in the darkness
Believing the night is the day?

What kind of world do you live in?
Is it blurred, distorted, and grey?
Where have you gone? I can't find you.
You seem to have drifted away.

Farewell visit

The day before the bulldozers moved in,
Grandpa took me across town by bus
To see the terraced house
Where he lived as a boy.

He pointed out where the standpipe was
And told me about the copper in the yard,
How he and his brothers shared a tin bath
Once a week.

He showed me where the privy stood
And the shed where they kept the coal
For the range on which his mother cooked
For a family of eight.

The house itself was empty,
Stripped bare, its windows boarded.
But in the yard
We found the remains of a mangle.

As we walked back to the bus-stop,
Grandpa peopled the street with his memories.

Beneath the bridge

Once, when Gran was a girl,
A river flowed
Between these banks
Its waters fresh and clear.

Now, the river bed
Is dried and cracked.
No water flows.
Instead,
Beneath the bridge,
A dirt-stained mattress
Leaks its stuffing
And plastic bags
Spew pools of rubbish.

Over the bridge,
Where Gran stood throwing sticks
Into the swirling current,
A stream of traffic roars,
Oblivious.

Then and Now

In the old days,
It took you a week
To travel from the south coast
To the Scottish border.

Now, a journey
That once took seven days
Takes less than seven hours.

In the old days,
Your journey took you
At a horse's pace
Over wooded hills
Of oak and ash and elm,
Between green fields
Where sheep and cattle grazed.

Today,
On concrete highways,
Carved at such a cost,
We race in frantic haste
From one vast conurbation
To the next,
Speed our only thought.

The landscape flashes past,
Disappearing.

Where is the forest?

Where is the forest?
cried the animals.
Where are the trees?

We needed the wood,
said the people.
Wood to make fires.
Wood to build houses.
We cut it down.

Where is the forest?
cried the animals.
Where are the trees?

We needed the land,
said the people.
Land for our cattle.
Land for our roads.
We cut it down.

Where is the forest?
cried the animals.
Where is our home?

Gone, whispered the wind.
Gone. Gone. Gone.

The Recycling Rap

Listen to me, children. Hear what I say.
We've got to start recycling. It's the only way
To save this planet for future generations –
The name of the game is reclamation.
You've got to start recycling. You know it makes sense.
You've got to start recycling. Stop sitting on the fence.
No more pussyfooting. No more claptrap.
Get yourself doing the recycling rap.

Come on and start recycling. Start today
By saving old newspapers, not throwing them away.
Don't just take them and dump them on the tip,
Tie them in a bundle and put them in the skip.

Get collecting, protecting the future's up to you.
Save all your old glass bottles and your jam jars too.
Take them to the bottle bank, then at the factory
The glass can be recycled, saving energy.

Don't chuck away that empty drink can.
Remember what I said. Start recycling, man.
Wash it, squash it, squeeze it flat and thin.
Take it to the Save-A-Can and post it in.

Listen to me, children. Hear what I say.
We've got to start recycling. It's the only way
To save this planet for future generations –
The name of the game is reclamation.
You've got to start recycling. You know it makes sense.
You've got to start recycling. Stop sitting on the fence.
No more pussyfooting. No more claptrap.
Get yourself doing the recycling rap.

Walls

All my life
I have walked on walls.

When I was little,
I stepped carefully,
Clutching my mother's hand tightly.

Later, I skipped happily along,
Secure in the knowledge
That if I fell
She would be there to pick me up
And console me.

As a student,
I strode purposefully
Towards my goal,
Masking my insecurity
With a show of confidence.

Next, surefooted,
I trod the walls I built,
Only gradually becoming aware
That the foundations
Were not as concrete as I thought.

Now, I walk slowly,
Tiptoeing along the battlements,
Fully conscious
How tightrope thin my path is.

Only one race

From start to finish
there is only one race.
Some glide effortlessly along smooth tracks
cushioned by prosperity.
Some stumble and fall
before even the first hurdle.
Others drop out at various intervals
as a result of poverty, sickness or war.
Most of us follow a zigzag course
we could not help but choose,
gradually running out of steam.

What is time?

A spool of film unwinding,
disappearing into the distance
like the dot on a TV screen.

The ceaseless ticking of a metronome
beating out the pulse of the future.

A computer code for unlocking
the order of events.

The graph on which
we measure out our memories
and calculate our dreams.

Superstition

Overnight,
The cracks in the pavement
Must have moved.
Today,
I could not avoid
Stepping on them.
What will tomorrow bring?